Intermediate
Vocabulary

B J THOMAS

LONGMAN

Pearson Education Limited,
Edinburgh Gate, Harlow,
Essex CM20 2JE, England

© B J Thomas 1986

This (revised) edition published by Longman Group Limited 1995
Fifth impression 1999

ISBN 0-17-557127-9

Illustrations by Chris Doyle, Dave Remnant

Printed in Malaysia, LSP

W 428 THO

Contents

Introduction

Intermediate Vocabulary is for students who already have a reasonable command of the basic structures of English and who now wish to expand their vocabulary. It can be used both in the classroom and at home. It gives invaluable assistance to students preparing for English examinations.

To the student

Intermediate Vocabulary presents new words from a wide variety of topic and language areas. Varied and enjoyable exercises, such as gap filling and word building, guide students in using the new words.

Learners studying on their own should avoid simply going through the book 'filling in the blanks'. Exercises should be done at intervals as a supplement to other materials, and students should give themselves time to practise and use what they have learnt before going on to learn more. It is not enough simply to complete the exercises and understand the new words encountered. Learners must actually use the words in conversation, composition or letters before they can feel that these words are truly a part of their active vocabulary. Although it is chiefly aimed at the intermediate student, advanced students will find this book useful to test and practise their vocabulary, as well as to fill in any gaps in their knowledge.

To the teacher

Intermediate Vocabulary is divided into different sections, each comprising a wide variety of exercises in which target words are contextualised. *Dictionary Practice* is provided in the first section. *Topics* and *Mini Topics* contain words and phrases in topic areas, such as sport or education, and include items useful for students writing about or discussing a particular topic. The fourth and fifth sections, *Related Word Groups* and *Word Building*, introduce new words and practise skills such as deducing meaning, word building and word transformation. The sixth section, *Specialised Vocabulary*, is intended for more advanced students, as an introduction to areas of language outside those they will have encountered so far in their studies. These include formal words, slang, popular language, words used in newspaper headlines, abbreviations, classified advertisements, shortened words and American words. There is also a section on the *British Isles*. The section, *Problem Pairs* is intended as a reference section to be turned to as and when problems arise with a particular pair of words. *Word Games* provides practice in spelling and vocabulary through a variety of interesting games and puzzles.

Information 'boxes' are found throughout the book, providing interesting facts about words and their meanings.

Intermediate Vocabulary can be used in a variety of ways. Exercises can be done as pair or group activities in class, leading to a discussion, writing activity or other creative task. Alternatively, exercises can be done as homework, with the aid of the key and a dictionary, in preparation for a class discussion or work on a specific area of language. The book can also be used for revision and consolidation work.

Dictionary Practice

What do you want from a dictionary? And how good is yours? Below is a list of things you find out in dictionaries. In column A, next to each item first put a number from 1 to 10 according to how important it is to you . 1 = most important; 10 = least important. Then look at *your* dictionary and see whether all these items can be found in it. In column B, write a number from 1 to 10 according to how good you think *your* dictionary is. 1 = very good; 10 = poor.

	A	B
illustrations		
list of irregular verbs		
help with the pronunciation and stress of each word		
British and American spelling		
clear explanations of word meanings		
useful introduction at the front		
examples of how the words are used (especially verbs)		
useful information and appendices at the back		
key to phonetic symbols		
list of useful abbreviations		

Use a good dictionary to do the following exercises. If you like, you can try to do them without help first, but check your answers in a dictionary afterwards.

Pronunciation

1   Divide the following words into three groups according to whether the vowel sound is pronounced /ʊ/ as in 'pull', /uː/ as in 'June' or /ʌ/ as in 'shut'.

wood	**good**	**food**	**book**	**soon**
school	**flood**	**look**	**blood**	**foot**

2   Divide the following words into three groups according to whether the vowel sound is pronounced /ɜː/ as in 'term', 'burn', /aː/ as in 'start', 'father' or /ɔː/ as in 'short', 'course'.

first	**world**	**heart**	**fast**	**lord**
warm	**taught**	**learn**	**hard**	**calm**
court	**laugh**	**turn**	**sort**	**word**

3   In each three-word group below circle the **two** words which have the same-sounding underlined parts.

e.g.   w<u>a</u>tch (m<u>a</u>tch) (c<u>a</u>tch)   (h<u>o</u>me) h<u>o</u>nest (h<u>i</u>ll)

s<u>e</u>lf w<u>o</u>lf ha<u>l</u>f	happ<u>y</u> rel<u>y</u> catastrophe
foll<u>ow</u> sh<u>ow</u> all<u>ow</u>	s<u>y</u>stem m<u>y</u>stery ps<u>y</u>chology
<u>u</u>ncle <u>u</u>nion <u>u</u>niversity	th<u>ough</u> r<u>ough</u> t<u>ough</u>
<u>ch</u>emical <u>ch</u>aracter <u>ch</u>annel	rec<u>ei</u>ve r<u>eig</u>n s<u>ei</u>ze

Stress

Mark the stressed syllable in each word below.

e.g. 'happiness guaran'tee en'joyable

coffee	employer	modern	admire
payee	employee	modernity	admirable
visit	advertise	modernisation	admiration
forget	advertisement	attention	infamous

Spelling

1   Finish the spelling of the words below with the correct ending -er, -or, or -ar.

teenag-	auth-	equat-	speak-	trait-
calend-	soldi-	lectur-	burgl-	nucle-
surviv-	vend-	muscul-	wait-	doll-

2   In the word-groups below finish the spelling of the words with the correct items from those above each group.

-ei   -ie

p-ce	rec-ve	rel-f	n-ce	w-gh
c-ling	pr-st	dec-ve	s-ze	for-gn

-ance -ence

appear-	correspond-	guid-	insur-	occurr-
innoc-	acquaint-	viol-	adolesc-	alli-

Meaning

1   Divide each of the following word lists into two equal groups below the correct headings above each list.

seats   **on the floor**

sofa	mat	parquet	throne	pew
bench	rug	lino	stool	carpet

clothing materials   **metals**

iron	steel	denim	tin	corduroy	silk
tweed	lead	velvet	suede	copper	gold

2   Each item on the left normally contains one of the items on the right. Make the correct pairs.

hangar	hearse	revolver	spectators
holster	reservoir	rubbish	coffin
dustbin	grandstand	water	aircraft

3   Each of the words below can be used as a noun and also, with a completely different meaning, as a verb. Give a simple example of each.

e.g. **park**: We played tennis in the park. I parked my car.

type	**sentence**	**train**	**state**	**stick**

Word Parts

1   Give the plural of these nouns.

potato   stratum   deer   crisis   shelf
thesis   chateau   thief   sheep   phenomenon

2   Make compound nouns or adjectives, using the word on the left as the first part, to fit the meanings given.

e.g. **head** (car front light) Answer: head-lamp

foot   (having aching feet)
            (sound of someone walking)

dog   (person given all the hard, boring work)
            (exhausted, worn out)

sea   (ill because of ship's motion)
            (plant growing in the sea)

Word Use

1   Complete these sentences with 'is' or 'are'.

(a)   All her furniture _____ Italian.
(b)   What _____ the police like in your country?
(c)   I'm afraid the news _____ bad.
(d)   Public transport _____ getting expensive.
(e)   The people next door _____ from Australia.
(f)   Billiards _____ a popular indoor game.
(g)   Accommodation in Tokyo _____ very expensive.
(h)   His clothes _____ always trendy.

2   Finish each incomplete sentence below so that it means the same as the sentence above it.

e.g. I regret doing it.
        I wish ... (Answer: I wish I hadn't done it.)

She advised them not to go there.
She discouraged ...
I begged her to help me.
I pleaded ...
We managed to finish in time.
We succeeded ...
They didn't allow him to leave.
They prevented ...

Topics

Air Travel

At the airport

1   Put each of the following words or phrases in its correct place in the passage below.

departure lounge	immigration officer	check	runway
departure gate	security guard	board	on board
departures board	excess baggage	check in	duty free
hand luggage	conveyor belt	taxi	passengers
announcement	check-in desk	trolley	take off
security check			

When you travel by air you have to get to the airport early in order to (a) _____ about an hour before your flight. If you have a lot of luggage, you can put it in a (b) _____ and push it to the (c) _____, where someone will (d) _____ your ticket and weigh your luggage. If you have (e) _____, it can be expensive. Your heavy luggage is put on a (f) _____ and carried away. A light bag is classed as (g) _____ and you can take it with you on to the plane An (h) _____ looks at your passport and a (i) _____ checks your hand luggage before you go into the (j) _____ to wait till your flight is called. If you want to, you can buy some cheap (k) _____ goods here. Then you see on the (l) _____ or you hear an (m) _____ that you must (n) _____ your plane. You go through the (o) _____, then there is sometimes a (p) _____ before you actually enter the plane. When all the (q) _____ are (r) _____, and when the captain and his crew are ready in the cockpit, the plane begins to (s) _____ to the end of the (t) _____. Finally, permission is received from the control tower and the plane moves faster and faster in order to (u) _____.

In the air

2   Instructions as above.

headphones	seat belts	aisle	land
turbulence	cabin crew	airliner	

Flying is fun. I like being in a big (a) _____ with the (b) _____ (stewards and stewardesses) looking after me. They walk up and down the (c) _____ bringing meals and drinks; and if the flight is going through some (d) _____, they warn everybody that it might be bit bumpy and ask us to fasten our (e) _____. On a long flight I like listening to music through the (f) _____ available to all passengers, and sometimes I have a sleep. I enjoy it all so much that I never want the plane to (g) _____.

3   Put one of the following words in each space in the sentences below.

through   at   to   off   in   on   for   by

(a)   We decided to go _____ plane.
(b)   When do we take _____?
(c)   First you must go _____ customs and immigration.
(d)   You'd better ask _____ the information desk.
(e)   His friend went _____ the airport with him to see him _____.
(f)   You must check _____ at 10.30.
(g)   Put your luggage _____ a trolley.
(h)   He looked _____ my passport.

Bank Accounts

Opening an account

1   Put each word or phrase in the group below in its correct place in the following passage.

formalities   open   account   bank charges
overdraft   branch   fill in

It's very simple to (a) _____ a bank (b) _____ in Britain. There are very few
(c) _____. Just go to your local (d) _____, (e) _____ a few forms, and that's it.
You will probably only have to pay (f) _____ if there is no money in your account
or if you borrow money from the bank, in other words if you have an (g) _____.

Current and deposit accounts

2   Instructions as above.

notice   current   cheque   withdraw   deposit   interest

For regular everyday use most people prefer a (a) _____ account. This normally
earns no (b) _____ but you are given a (c) _____ book, which makes shopping
and paying bills very easy. A (d) _____ account earns interest but it's not so easy to
(e) _____ your money. You sometimes have to give a week's (f) _____.

Using your account

3   Instructions as above.

balance   deposit   withdrawal   standing order   statement

At regular intervals, perhaps monthly, you will receive a (a) _____ from the bank,
giving details of each (b) _____ (money you put in) and (c) _____ (money you
take out). If you're not sure how much money you have in your account, you can
just go to your bank and ask what your (d) _____ is. If you have to make a regular
payment, like rent, you can ask the bank to pay this amount for you automatically.
This arrangement is called a (e) _____.

Spending

4 Instructions as above.

expenditure	counterfoil	income	keep a record
crossed	overdrawn	cash	

Some people spend more money than they receive. In other words, their (a) _____ is greater than their (b) _____. If you take more money out of the bank than you have in your account, you are (c) _____. To (d) _____ of your spending, it's a good idea when you write a cheque to fill in the (e) _____, which stays in the book. Most cheques are (f) _____ cheques, which means that no one else can (g) _____ them. They must be paid into someone's account.

5 Put one of the following words or phrases in each space in the sentences.

out of   from   for   at   in   to

(a) He borrowed £10 _____ his father.
(b) She filled _____ the cheque.
(c) I asked _____ my balance.
(d) I prefer a current account _____ a deposit account.
(e) You'll get a statement _____ regular intervals.
(f) He took £100 _____ his bank.
(g) He withdrew £100 _____ his bank.

TRADE NAMES

Businesses and shops often choose unusual names with unconventional spelling to attract attention. From the names below, can you find the snack bar, stationers, shoe-repairers, bed shop, dry cleaners and travel agency?

Kwick Kleen	Sleepeezee	Nu-a-Gane
Mr. Sam Widge	Just Write	Rite Flite

Books and Reading

Kinds of book

1   Match each kind of book on the right below with the kind of material you would normally find in it, on the left.

(a)   maps
(b)   exercises and diagrams etc. for school study
(c)   meanings of words
(d)   information about a subject
(e)   an exciting story of crime or adventure
(f)   instructions, e.g. on how to maintain, repair and use a car
(g)   tourist information and advice about a place or country
(h)   a list of important, famous people and details of their lives

guidebook
dictionary
manual
atlas
thriller
textbook
Who's Who
encyclopaedia

Reading

2   Put each of the following words in its correct place in the passage below.

fine	bookworm	browse	bibliography
footnotes	reviews	illustrations	borrow
glossary	published		

I love books. I love to read. I'm a real (a) _____, and I love to (b) _____ in bookshops, just looking briefly at one book after another. I look at the (c) _____, the photos or drawings. If there are foreign or technical words in the book, I look at the (d) _____ at the back for their meanings (unless they're explained in (e) _____ at the bottom of the pages) and I look at the (f) _____, also at the back, which is a list of other books on the same subject. And I use the library a lot. I (g) _____ two or three books a week, and I have to pay a (h) _____ if I return them late. Friends often recommend books to me, and I also read book (i) _____ in the newspapers. I don't always agree with them, but anyway they let me know what new books are being (j) _____.

3   Explain the difference between ...

(a)   contents page and index
(b)   bookshop and library
(c)   author and publisher
(d)   lend and borrow
(e)   biography and autobiography
(f)   fiction, non-fiction and reference books

4   Put one of the following words in each space in the sentences below.

by   from   in   up   at   on

(a)   I borrowed this book _____ the library.
(b)   The index is _____ the back of the book.
(c)   There are footnotes _____ the bottom of the page.
(d)   I read it _____ a book.
(e)   You'll have to look _____ the meaning _____ a dictionary.
(f)   'Hamlet' is _____ Shakespeare.
(g)   The librarian said the book was _____ the top shelf.

Cars

Parts of a Car

1   Next to each letter in the pictures below, write the name of the car-part it illustrates from the following list.

windscreen wipers   clutch (pedal)   seat belt   tyre
accelerator (pedal)   brake (pedal)   headrest   aerial
rear-view mirror   exhaust pipe   bumper   boot
steering wheel   windscreen   bonnet   wheel
number plate   headlights   gear lever   engine
dashboard

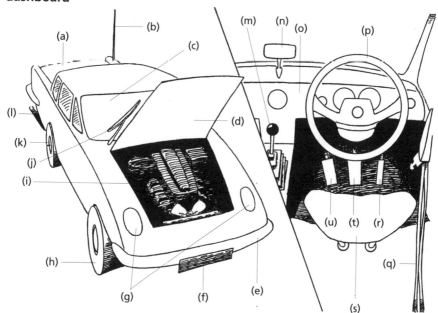

Cars and driving

2   Put each of the following words or phrases in its correct place in the sentences below.

overtake   indicate   fuel consumption   rear
petrol tank   vehicle   performance   body
instruments   reverse   mpg (miles per gallon)

(a)   The amount of petrol a car uses is called the _____ and it is measured in _____. The petrol goes in the _____.

(b)   The way a car behaves (speed, brakes, acceleration etc.) is called the car's _____.

(c)   We can talk about the back of a _____ (car, bus, lorry etc.) but more often we use the word _____.

(d)   The speedometer, fuel gauge, and so on are called _____.

(e)   To _____ means to pass another vehicle going in the same direction.

(f)   If you have to go backwards, you _____.

(g)   The outside surface of the car, made of metal or fibreglass, is called the _____.

(h)   Make sure you _____ before turning left or right.

Cinema and Films

A visit to the cinema

1   Put each of the following words in its correct place in the passage below.

cinema	foyer	aisle	trailer	cartoon
critic	auditorium	poster	row	screen
horror	performance	review		

Fiona and I went to the (a) _____ the other day to see 'Devil' at the Odeon. The (b) _____ by the Daily Express (c) _____ was good, and we decided to go to the 8 o'clock (d) _____. When I arrived, Fiona was waiting for me in the (e) _____, looking at a (f) _____ for 'Devil' on the wall. We went into the (g) _____ and sat down. I don't like to be too close to the (h) _____ and I usually sit in the back (i) _____ if possible, and I prefer a seat on the (j) _____ so I can stretch my legs. Before the main film there was a Mickey Mouse (k) _____, then a (l) _____ for the following week's film. 'Devil' was a (m) _____ film and I was quite terrified, but Fiona thought it was funny.

A film review

2   Instructions as above.

documentary	location	role	director	cast
performance	studio	critical	box office	plot

Marlon Brando is a superb actor and in 'On the Waterfront' he gave his finest (a) _____. It is his best-known (b) _____. The (c) _____ also included Eva Marie Saint and Karl Malden and the film's (d) _____, Elia Kazan, never made a better film. Parts of the film were shot in the (e) _____ in Hollywood, but a lot was made on (f) _____ in the streets of New York, which makes it at times like a (g) _____. The critics loved the film but it was not only a (h) _____ success. It was a great (i) _____ success as well, and made an enormous profit. The (j) _____ is about a young man's attempt to be a boxing champion.

3   Put one of the following words in each space in the sentences below.

to   in   on   at   for

(a)   It wasn't made _____ location.
(b)   It was made _____ the studio.
(c)   Is there a good firm _____ tonight?
(d)   What's _____ _____ the Odeon?
(e)   He likes to sit _____ the aisle.
(f)   It happened _____ the beginning of the film.
(g)   There was a trailer _____ the next week's film.
(h)   Let's go _____ the cinema.
(i)   This film is based _____ a book.
(j)   I like to sit _____ the back.
(k)   She prefers to sit _____ the front.
(l)   We were shown _____ our seats _____ the third row.
(m) Sometimes the cast list comes _____ the end of the film.

Doctors and Hospitals

Medical staff and patients

1   Match each of these people with the correct definition below.

patient	casualty	nurse
psychiatrist	out-patient	midwife
in-patient	surgeon	medical student
specialist		general practitioner

(a)   an ordinary doctor
(b)   someone who looks after sick people in hospital
(c)   person who helps people with mental problems
(d)   sick person receiving treatment
(e)   sick person who has to stay in hospital
(f)   sick person who has to visit the hospital regularly for treatment
(g)   someone who operates on sick people
(h)   person badly injured in an accident, fire, war
(i)   person who helps at the birth of a baby
(j)   person who studies to be a doctor
(k)   person who specializes in one area of medical treatment

Doctors' surgeries and hospitals

2   Put each of the following words in its correct place in the passage below.

thermometer	prescription	operation	chemist
stethoscope	receptionist	appointment	ward
temperature	examine	treatment	pulse
waiting room	symptoms		

When I go to the doctor, I tell the (a) _____ my name and take a seat in the
(b) _____. My doctor is very busy so I have to make an (c) _____ before I go to
see him. He asks me what's wrong with me, I tell him the (d) _____ of my illness,
for example high temperature, difficulty in breathing, or pains, and then he will
usually (e) _____ me. He'll listen to my heart with his (f) _____, he'll hold my
wrist to feel my (g) _____, he'll take my (h) _____ with his (i) _____.
The problem is usually something simple and he might give me a (j) _____ for
some medicine, which I take to the (k) _____. Of course, if I needed more serious
(l) _____, I'd have to go to hospital. There I'd be put in a bed in a (m) _____
with 10 or 20 other people. If there were something seriously wrong with me,
I might need an (n) _____.

3   Put one of the following words in each space in the sentences below.

from   on   with   in   to   for   of

(a)   He was operated _____ yesterday.
(b)   She was taken _____ hospital.
(c)   He suffered _____ bad headaches.
(d)   I have a pain _____ my back.
(e)   What's wrong _____ you?
(f)   He died _____ cancer.
(g)   She got worse so they sent _____ a doctor.

Education

1   Put each of the following words or phrases in its correct space in the passage below.

state	terms	seminar	degree	co-educational
private	primary	tutorial	graduate	nursery school
grant	secondary	lecture	break up	compulsory
fees	academic			

When children are two or three years old, they sometimes go to a (a) _____, where they learn simple games and songs. Their first real school is called a (b) _____ school. In Britain children start this school at the age of five. The (c) _____ year in Britain begins in September and is divided into three (d) _____. Schools (e) _____ for the summer holiday in July. (f) _____ education begins at the age of about eleven, and most schools at this level are (g) _____, which means boys and girls study together in the same classes. In Britain education is (h) _____ from five to 16 years of age, but many children choose to remain at school for another two or three years after 16 to take higher exams. Most children go to (i) _____ schools, which are maintained by the government or local education authorities, but some children go to (j) _____ schools, which can be very expensive. University courses normally last three years and then students (k) _____, which means they receive their (l) _____. At university, teaching is by (m) _____ (an individual lesson between a teacher and one or two students), (n) _____ (a class of students discussing a subject with a teacher), (o) _____ (when a teacher gives a prepared talk to a number of students) and of course private study. Most people who receive a university place are given a (p) _____ by the government to help pay their (q) _____ and living expenses.

2   Explain the difference between ...
(a)   to sit an exam and to set an exam
(b)   to take an exam and to pass an exam
(c)   compulsory and voluntary
(d)   to educate and to bring up
(e)   a pupil and a student

3   Put one of the following words in each space in the sentences below.

up   to   of   at   by   from   in   into

(a)   Which school do you go _____?
(b)   He left school _____ the age _____ 18.
(c)   The summer term ends _____ July.
(d)   She's not at home, she's _____ school,
(e)   She goes _____ Sussex University.
(f)   His lecture was divided _____ four parts.
(g)   School breaks _____ next Friday.
(h)   He is now _____ university.
(i)   She is _____ the same class as her brother.
(j)   Students usually receive a grant _____ the state.
(k)   They're given a grant _____ the state.

Elections and Government

Elections

1 Put each of the following words or phrases in its correct place in the passage below.

election campaign	**support**	**polling day**	**opinion poll**	**vote**
polling station	**predict**	**ballot box**	**candidate**

People sometimes try to (a) _____ the result of an election weeks before it takes place. Several hundred people are asked which party they prefer, and their answers are used to guess the result of the coming election. This is called an (b) _____. Meanwhile each party conducts its (c) _____ with meetings, speeches, television commercials and party members going from door to door encouraging people to (d) _____ their party. In Britain everyone over 18 is eligible to (e) _____. The place where people go to vote in an election is called a (f) _____ and the day of the election is often known as (g) _____. The voters put their votes in a (h) _____ and later they are counted. The (i) _____ with the most votes is then declared the winner.

Government

2 Instructions as above.

cabinet	**alliance**	**right-wing**	**prime minister**	**one-party states**
coalition	**majority**	**left-wing**	**opposition**	**split**

In most countries, except (a) _____, there are several different political parties. The one with the (b) _____ of seats normally forms the government, and the parties which are against the government are called the (c) _____. Sometimes no single party wins enough seats, and several parties must combine together in a (d) _____ to form a government. The principal ministers in the government form a group called the (e) _____. The leader of this group, and of the government, is the (f) _____. Of course, there are many different kinds of parties and governments. A socialist or communist party is often described as (g) _____. A conservative party on the other hand, is usually said to be (h) _____. Political situations are always changing. Sometimes in a party or between two parties there is a big argument or deep difference of opinion. This is called a (i) _____. When, on the other hand, two parties work together, this is sometimes called an (j) _____.

3 Explain the difference between ...
(a) pro- and anti-
(b) an election and a referendum

4 Put one of the following words in each space in the sentences below.

with   for   against   to   in   between

(a) I voted _____ the Liberal candidate.
(b) Put your voting papers _____ the ballot box.
(c) He's very right-wing, so he's _____ the socialists.
(d) She belongs _____ the Communist Party.
(e) The Liberals formed an alliance _____ the Social Democrats.
(f) There's a split _____ the two parties.
(g) There's a split _____ the party.

Flats and Houses

Renting a flat

1   Put each of the following words or phrases in its correct position in the passage below.

deposit	fee	flat	advertisements	accommodation agency
landlord	rent	block	self-contained	references

The first thing I had to do in Belfast was find somewhere to live, if possible a small, one-bedroomed (a) _____. I didn't want to share a kitchen or toilet; I wanted to be independent in my own (b) _____ place. I decided I could pay a (c) _____ of £50 a week. I couldn't find what I wanted in the newspaper (d)_____ so I went to an (e) _____. They offered me a nice place. It was in a modern (f) _____ on the third floor. I had to pay the agency a (g) _____, and the (h) _____ wanted a big (i) _____ and (j) _____ from my employer and bank manager.

Buying a house

2   Instructions as above.

condition	detached	removals	cramped	semi-detached	builder
spacious	surveyor	architect	terraced	estate-agent	

Tony and Sheila's first home was a (a) _____ house, one of a line of houses all connected. But several years later when they had a small child, they found it rather (b) _____ for three people. They wanted something more (c) _____ and so decided to move. They went to an (d) _____ and looked at details of the houses he had to offer. They looked at a (e) _____ house (one of a pair attached to each other), liked it, and asked a (f) _____ to inspect it for them. He said that it was in good (g) _____, and they therefore decided to buy it. Luckily they sold their house quickly and soon a (h) _____ firm was taking all their furniture and other possessions to their new home. But already, after a couple of years, they are hoping to move again. Tony's business is doing well and they want to get an (i) _____ to design a modern, (j) _____ house for them, and a (k) _____ to build it.

3   Explain the difference between ...
(a)   a landlord and a tenant
(b)   a house and a bungalow
(c)   ground floor and first floor

4   Put one of the following words in each space in the sentences below.

for   at   in   on   of   into   with

(a)   She wanted a place _____ her own.
(b)   He'll move _____ tomorrow.
(c)   He'll move _____ his new flat tomorrow.
(d)   I share the kitchen _____ three other people.
(e)   The landlord asked the tenant _____ more rent.
(f)   My flat is _____ the top floor.
(g)   My flat is _____ a modern block.
(h)   The house is _____ good condition.
(i)   I looked _____ advertisements _____ the newspaper.
(j)   She pays a rent _____ £90 a week.

Food and Restaurants

Eating out

1   Put each of the following words or phrases in its correct place in the passage.

recipe   fast food   eat out   dish   bill   cookery books
menu   take-away   waiter   snack   tip   ingredients

I'm a terrible cook. I've tried hard but it's no use. I've got lots of (a) _____, I choose
a (b) _____ I want to cook, I read the (c) _____, I prepare all the necessary
(d) _____ and follow the instructions. But the result is terrible, and I just have a
sandwich or some other quick (e) _Snack_. So I often (f) _o_____. I don't like grand
restaurants. It's not the expense, it's just that I don't feel at ease in them. First the
(g) _____ gives me a (h) _____ which I can't understand because it's complicated
and has lots of foreign words. At the end of the meal when I pay the (i) _____
I never know how much to leave as a (j) _____. I prefer (k) _____ places, like
hamburger shops where you pay at once and sit down and eat straightaway. And I
like (l) _____ places, where you buy a meal in a special container and take it home.

Entertaining at home

2   Instructions as above.

vegetarian   crockery   side dish   diet
main course   napkin   sink   starter
washing up   dessert   cutlery   entertaining

Maureen often gives dinner parties at home. She loves (a) _____. She lays the table:
puts the (b) _____ in the right places, sets out the plates and puts a clean white
(c) _____ at each place. For the meal itself, she usually gives her guests some kind
of (d) _____ first, for example soup or melon. Next comes the (e) _____, which is
usually meat (unless some of her guests are (f) _____ or if they're on a special
(g) _____) with a (h) _____ of salad. For (i) _____ it's usually fruit or ice-cream,
and then coffee. When everyone has gone home, she must think about doing the
(j) _____, as in the kitchen the (k) _____ is full of dirty (l) _____.

3   Explain the difference between …
(a)   a buffet and a banquet   (c)   a chef and a caterer
(b)   overcooked, undercooked and raw   (d)   a café and a canteen

4   Put one of the following words in each space in the sentences below.

to   at   down   of   for   out   in   up

(a)   I asked _____ the menu.
(b)   I like to eat _____.
(c)   He took _____ my order.
(d)   I prefer a simple café _____ a big restaurant.
(e)   I like to go _____ self-service places.
(f)   Let's invite the Smiths _____ dinner.
(g)   I looked _____ the menu.
(h)   I'm very fond _____ Chinese food
(i)   Could you help me set _____ the plates?
(j)   Put the used cutlery _____ the sink.
(k)   I'll wash them _____ later.

Gambling, Smoking and Drinking

Gambling

1   Put each of the following words or phrases in its correct place in the passage below.

fortune	wreck	punters	compulsive gamblers
broke	betting	casino	games of chance
odds	bookmakers		

Some people are (a) _____ which means that they simply cannot stop (b) _____ on horses or playing (c) _____. It can be like a disease. If you're lucky, you can win a (d) _____ but if you're unlucky it can (e) _____ your life. And most people are unlucky. The (f) _____ are always against the gambler. At the race course it is the (g)_____ who win and the (h) _____ who lose. From a game of roulette in the (i) _____, the house makes a profit, the gambler often goes (j) _____.

Smoking

2   Instructions as above.

| craving | packet | chain-smoke | stained | put out |
| harmful | addiction | antisocial | fatal | ash trays |

To many people smoking is not just a pleasure, it is an (a) _____. They need it, depend on it, can't stop it. If they haven't smoked for some hours, they feel a (b) _____ for a cigarette. They often (c) _____, which means they light another cigarette immediately they have (d) _____ the one before. Smoking is often considered (e) _____, since many people don't like the smell of cigarettes or the sight of the smoker's (f) _____ fingers or (g) _____ full of cigarette-ends. Above all, smoking is (h) _____ to health and in many countries a warning is printed on every (i) _____ of cigarettes. Scientists have proved that there is a link between smoking and a disease which can be (j) _____, cancer

Drinking

3   Instructions as above.

| sociable | sip | soft drinks | sober | alcoholics |
| spirits | tipsy | teetotallers | drunk | hangover |

Drinking habits vary. Some people don't drink alcohol at all, just (a) _____ like fruit juice. They are called (b) _____. Others like to (c) _____ a glass of wine slowly, just to be (d) _____. Others like to drink glass after glass of beer, or possibly (e) _____ such as whisky, brandy or vodka. Soon they become (f) _____ and if they continue, they'll get (g) _____ and wake up the next morning with a bad (h) _____. Some people are dependent on alcohol. They can't do without it. They are (i) _____. One thing is certain. If you drive, you shouldn't drink. Stay (j) _____.

Industry and Agriculture

Industry

1   Put each of the following words in its correct place in the passage below.

produce   **shipyards**   **products**   **export**   **natural resources**
markets   **economy**   **boom**   **plants**   **import**
slump

The health of a big, developed country's (a) _____ depends largely on its industry.
Factories have to keep busy. They must (b) _____ and sell their (c) _____ in large
quantities. (d) _____ must make and sell ships; car (e) _____ must make and sell
cars. A period of industrial success, when everything goes well and large profits are
made, is called a (f) _____. On the other hand a period when there is not much
industrial activity is called a (g) _____. To maintain a high level of production is not
simple. For example Japan, a very successful industrialised country, has very few
(h) _____ such as oil or coal, and has to (i) _____ them from other countries in
order to keep its industries going, and thus to supply needs at home and also to
(j) _____ its goods to its overseas (k) _____.

Agriculture

2   Instructions as above.

livestock   **crops**   **agricultural**   **dams**   **fertilizers**
harvest   **irrigate**   **self-sufficient**   **fertile**   **farmers**

A country which wishes to be (a) _____ in food will encourage its (b) _____ to
produce as much as possible so that it will not be dependent on food imports. If
there is not much rain, (c) _____ must be built on rivers to provide water to
(d) _____ the land. If the land is not naturally rich, chemical (e) _____ must be
used to make it (f) _____. Then (g) _____ (of wheat, rice etc.) will grow, the
(h) _____ will be good, and in addition the (i) _____ (cattle, sheep etc.) will have
grass to eat. If this does not happen, the (j) _____ sector of the country's economy
will suffer and the country will have to import food from abroad.

3   Explain the difference between ...
(a)   an oilfield and an oil refinery
(b)   a mine and a quarry
(c)   the producer and the consumer
(d)   to plough and to sow

4   Put one of the following words in each space in the sentences below.

in   to   on   from   of

(a)   Profits depend largely _____ production and sales.
(b)   There is a boom _____ shipbuilding.
(c)   The main export _____ Iran is oil.
(d)   This land suffers _____ lack of water.
(e)   Thailand is self-sufficient _____ rice.
(f)   Sweden exports wood _____ the UK.

International Relations

A summit meeting

1   Put each of the following words or phrases in its correct place in the passage below.

summit meeting	breakdown	leader	item	spokesperson
news conference	preliminary	settle	hold	agenda

The American President and the Russian (a) _____ have announced their intention to (b) _____ a (c) _____ in Vienna next month. The two countries have already had (d) _____ talks and decided on an (e) _____ for the meeting. The main (f) _____ will be a discussion about the nuclear arms situation. At a (g) _____ held in Washington yesterday a government (h) _____ told journalists that the unfortunate (i) _____ of last year's talks between the two countries had been caused by disagreements over arms. He said the Vienna meeting would be a chance for the two nations to (j) _____ their differences.

Diplomatic relations

2   Instructions as above.

diplomatic relations	ambassadors	split	embassies
in protest at	resume	links	break off

Neighbouring countries A and B had always had very good, close relations, but in 1992, owing to a disagreement over the exact location of the border between them, a (a) _____ began to develop. Finally, in 1994, (b) _____ military activity by country B near the border, country A announced its intention to (c) _____ (d) _____ with country B. Both countries withdrew their (e) _____ and the (f) _____ in the two countries were closed down. It is hoped that a solution will be found and that it will be possible to (g) _____ normal trade, cultural and diplomatic (h) _____ as soon as possible.

3   Put one of the following words in each space in the sentences below.

in   for   over   of   on   at   about   by

(a)   The French leader hasn't yet decided _____ a date _____ the meeting.
(b)   At a summit meeting each country is represented _____ its head of government.
(c)   The announcement was made _____ a news conference _____ Moscow.
(d)   The ambassadors had a discussion _____ the peace treaty.
(e)   The breakdown _____ the talks surprised everyone.
(f)   The American ambassador walked out of the meeting _____ protest _____ the Russian speech.
(g)   A spokeswoman said there was some disagreement _____ the agenda _____ the meeting.

Law and Order

An arrest

1 Put each of the following words in its correct place in the passage below.

theft	pleaded	fingerprints	witnesses	evidence	found
arrest	oath	investigate	sentence	charge	cell
detained	fine	court	magistrate	handcuff	

A policeman was sent to (a) _____ the disappearance of some property from a hotel. When he arrived, he found that the hotel staff had caught a boy in one of the rooms with a camera and some cash. When the policeman tried to (b) _____ the boy, he became violent and the policeman had to (c) _____ him. At the police station the boy could not give a satisfactory explanation for his actions and the police decided to (d) _____ him with the (e) _____ of the camera and cash. They took his (f) _____, locked him in a (g) _____, and (h) _____ him overnight. The next morning he appeared in (i) _____ before the (j) _____. He took an (k) _____ and (l) _____ not guilty. Two (m) _____, the owner of the property and a member of the hotel staff, gave (n) _____. After both sides of the case had been heard the boy was (o) _____ guilty. He had to pay a (p) _____ of £50 and he was given a (q) _____ of three months in prison suspended for two years.

Law and punishment

2 Instructions as above.

detective	plain clothes	jury	warders	coroner
verdict	solicitor	trial	inquest	death penalty

(a) If you want legal advice in Britain, you go to a _____.
(b) At the end of the _____, the judge ordered the twelve men and women of the _____ to retire and consider their _____, guilty or not guilty.
(c) Men or women who look after prisoners in prison are called prison officers or _____.
(d) If a person dies in unusual circumstances, an _____ is held at a special court, and the 'judge' is called a _____.
(e) A policeman who investigates serious crime is called a _____. He wears _____, not uniform.
(f) In some countries murderers are executed but other countries have abolished the _____.

3 Put one of the following words in each space in the sentences below.

before   in   to   of   with

(a) He's being kept _____ custody.
(b) He was sentenced _____ five years.
(c) She got a sentence _____ six months.
(d) He was accused _____ murder.
(e) She's been charged _____ theft.
(f) He appeared _____ court _____ handcuffs.
(g) They were brought _____ the judge.
(h) The jury reached a verdict _____ guilty.

Music

Classical music

1   Put each of the following words and phrases in its correct place in the passage below.

musicians	bow	string	conductor
instruments	score	keys	concert hall
audience	baton	bows	

While the (a) _____ was filling up and the (b) _____ were taking their seats, the (c) _____ were tuning their (d) _____. The famous (e) _____ entered. He gave the audience a low (f) _____, picked up his (g) _____, looked briefly at the (h) _____ which lay open in front of him, and raised his hands. The pianist placed her fingers ready over the (i) _____ of her piano. The (j) _____ section of the orchestra (violinists, cellists etc.) brought their (k) _____ up, ready to play. The concert was about to begin.

Popular music

2   Instructions as above.

group	vocalist	live	stage	number one
fans	concert	lyrics	top ten	recording studio

After the Beatles, The Rolling Stones have probably been the most successful (a) _____ in Britain. Most of their records have gone into the (b) _____ and they've had many at (c) _____. But their records have usually been made in a (d) _____ and I always wanted to hear them (e) _____ at a (f) _____. I wanted to see them perform on (g) _____ in front of thousands of excited (h) _____. And I did, at Earls Court in 1990. It was great. And Mick Jagger, the (i) _____, sang all the old favourites. I couldn't hear the (j) _____ very well because of the noise, but somehow it didn't matter.

3   Explain the difference between …
(a)   an orchestra and a band
(b)   percussion instruments and wind instruments
(c)   a concert and a rehearsal
(d)   a composer and a musician

4   Put one of the following words in each space in the sentences below.

by   in   at   on

(a)   What record is _____ number one?
(b)   Their new record is _____ the top ten.
(c)   This music was written _____ Chopin.
(d)   I haven't see this group _____ stage.
(e)   Who's the guitarist _____ that group?

Natural Disasters

Famine and flood

1 Put each of the following words or phrases in its correct place in the passage.

drought   **famine**   **starve**   **starvation**   **cut off**
helicopters   **drop**   **flood**   **drown**

If a country has no rain for a long time, this dry period is called a (a) _____.
In countries dependent on their agriculture, this can lead to a period of (b) _____,
when there is not enough food and people actually (c) _____ (die of hunger). They
die of (d) _____. When it rains very heavily and the land is under water, this is called
a (e) _____. In this situation people and animals can (f) _____. Sometimes
(g) _____ have to (h) _____ food supplies to people in areas which are (i) _____.

Earthquake and epidemic

2 Instructions as above.

medical teams   **trapped**   **epidemic**   **toll**   **outbreak**
rescue teams   **rubble**   **casualties**   **collapse**   **earthquake**

In some parts of the world, the ground shakes from time to time. This is called an
(a) _____ and if it's a bad one, the number of (b) _____ (dead and injured
people) is sometimes large. Buildings often (c) _____ and (d) _____ have to
search for people who are (e) _____ under the (f) _____. Sometimes water
supplies are affected and there is an (g) _____ of disease, called an (h) _____.
(i) _____ are sent by the government to help the sick. The death (j) _____ can
reach hundreds or even thousands.

Fire

3 Instructions as above.

on fire   **fire engine**   **under control**   **fireman**
put out   **fire brigade**   **overcome**   **arson**

During the night it was reported that a house was (a) _____. Someone phoned
the (b) _____ and a (c) _____ was sent to the house. One (d) _____ was
(e) _____ by smoke and taken to hospital, but in half an hour the fire was
(f) _____ and after another half hour it was finally (g) _____. At first the police
thought it was an accident, but later they found matches and a petrol can and
began to suspect (h) _____.

4 Put one of the following words in each space in the sentences below.

for   **in**   **of**   **to**   **from**   **off**   **under**   **by**

(a) Many people died _____ starvation.
(b) There are earthquakes in Japan _____ time _____ time.
(c) Food supplies are dropped _____ people whose homes are cut _____.
(d) Rescue teams searched _____ injured people.
(e) There was a drought _____ ten months _____ Central Africa.
(f) Many people were trapped _____ the rubble of the building which had collapsed.
(g) Medical teams were sent _____ the government.

Public Transport

1   Put each of the following words in its correct place in the passage below.

sliding doors	platform	conductor	fare	crew	cab
double-decker	bus stop	rush hour	tube	metro	lift
destination	inspector	subway	hail	check	tip
single-decker	taxi-rank	driver	coach	meter	rack
escalator					

A taxi, sometimes called a (a) _____, is the most comfortable way to travel. You
simply (b) _____ the taxi in the street or go to a (c) _____, where there are
several taxis waiting, for example at a station. At the end of your journey, you can
see how much the (d) _____ is by looking at the (e) _____. You add a
(f) _____ to this, and that's it. Very simple. But expensive!

What about taking a bus? If it has two floors, it's called a (g) _____ and you can
get a good view from the top. If it has only one floor, it's called a (h) _____. Most
buses have a two-person (i) _____: the (j) _____, who drives, of course, and the
(k) _____, who takes your money. Keep your ticket because an (l) _____ might
want to (m) _____ it. You catch a bus by waiting at a (n) _____. You can see
where a bus is going because the (o) _____ is written on the front. But try to
avoid the (p) _____.

Quicker than the bus is the underground (called the (q) _____ in London, the
(r) _____ in New York and the (s) _____ in Paris and many other cities). You buy
your ticket at the ticket-office. Go down to the (t) _____ on the (u) _____ or in
the (v) _____. The train comes. The (w) _____ open. You get on. You look at the
map of the underground system. Very simple.

For longer distances take a train or a long distance bus, usually called a (x) _____,
which is slower but cheaper. The train is very fast. Put your luggage on the
(y) _____ and sit and wait till you arrive.

2   Explain the difference between ...
(a) a carriage and a compartment
(b) a season ticket and a return ticket
(c) a bus driver and a bus conductor
(d) a train driver and a guard

3   Put one of the following words in each space in the sentences below.

for   off   at   in   on   from

(a) We went down _____ the lift.
(b) We met _____ the station.
(c) I waited 20 minutes _____ a bus.
(d) She had to queue _____ a bus.
(e) We must wait _____ the bus stop.
(f) She waited _____ the platform.
(g) The tube stops _____ every station.
(h) The conductor asked _____ our fares.
(i) We finally got _____ the bus _____ our destination.
(j) I'll meet you _____ the ticket office.
(k) Get your ticket _____ the machine.

Romance and Marriage

Romance

1   Put each of the following words or phrases in its correct place in the passage below.

date	approve	mature	attracted	romantic
keen	break off	go out	relationship	drift apart

Ann was a very (a) _____ girl who often dreamed of love and marriage. She was especially (b) _____ to a young man called Michael, who worked in the same office as she did, and he was very (c) _____ on her too. They became friendly and one day Michael asked her to go out with him. Their first (d) _____ was a visit to the cinema, and they both enjoyed the evening so much that they decided to (e) _____ together regularly. Michael was a bit untidy and rather young, and Ann's parents didn't (f) _____ of him at first, but Ann was a sensible, (g) _____ girl and they had confidence in her. For a year or so everything went well, but then somehow they slowly began to (h) _____, until finally they decided to (i) _____ their (j) _____.

Marriage

2   Put each of the following words in its correct place in the passage below.

bride	engaged	bridegroom	consent	wedding
civil	reception	honeymoon	propose	toast

One evening, although he was nervous, Joe decided to (a) _____ to his girlfriend, Linda. She accepted his proposal, they became (b) _____ and he gave her a ring. After a year they had saved enough money to get married (they were both over 18 so they did not need their parents' (c) _____). Some people have a religious ceremony with a priest, but Joe and Linda decided on a (d) _____ ceremony in a registry office. On the day of the (e) _____ Linda, the (f) _____, was very calm, but Joe, the (g) _____, was nervous. Afterwards, at the (h) _____, speeches were made and the guests drank a (i) _____ to the happy couple, who finally left for a (j) _____ in Spain.

3   Explain the difference between ...
(a)   to be fond of and to be in love with   (c)   a fiancé and a fiancée
(b)   separated and divorced   (d)   mother and mother-in-law

4   Put one of the following words in each space in the sentences below.

in   with   out   to   of

(a)   Bob and Leanne are going _____ together.
(b)   Bob is going _____ _____ Leanne.
(c)   He was too nervous to ask her _____.
(d)   She's very fond _____ him.
(e)   We drank a toast _____ their future happiness.
(f)   He fell _____ love _____ her at once.
(g)   He's getting married _____ Liz next month.
(h)   She's engaged _____ a policeman.
(i)   His parents don't approve _____ her.
(j)   Have confidence _____ me!

Shopping

Kinds of shop

1   What would you buy in the following shops?

florist's   greengrocer's   baker's
butcher's   tobacconist's   pet shop
grocer's   newsagent's   antique shop
stationer's

Going shopping

2   Put each of the following words or phrases in its correct place in the passage below.

cash desk	sales	tag	label	off-the-peg
refund	try on	fit	receipt	assistant
mail order	bargain	till	cashier	exchange

If you want to buy a ready-made (or we sometimes say (a) _____) jacket, first find the jackets in the shop and look at the (b) _____ inside to see the size, material and make. For the price, look at the price- (c) _____. To see if it will (d) _____ you, you can (e) _____ the jacket in front of a mirror. If necessary an (f) _____ will help you. You pay the (g) _____, who you will find at the (h) _____. He or she will take your money, put it in the (i) _____ and give you your change. Make sure you also get a (j) _____, which you should keep and bring back to the shop with the jacket if something is wrong with it and you want to (k) _____ it or ask for a (l) _____ of your money. In clothes shops you pay the fixed price, of course. You don't (m) _____. Or you can wait until the (n) _____, when many goods are reduced in price. If you don't like shops, you can stay at home, look at catalogues and newspaper advertisements and do your shopping by (o) _____.

3   Explain the difference between …
(a)   to overcharge and to undercharge
(b)   a shopkeeper and a shoplifter
(c)   shopping and window-shopping
(d)   a wholesaler and a retailer

4   Put one of the following words in each space in the sentences below.

in   on   for   with   at   by   inside   back

(a)   These jackets are reduced _____ price.
(b)   The assistant advised me to try the coat _____.
(c)   I want to look _____ the animals _____ the pet shop.
(d)   He bought many things _____ mail order.
(e)   There is normally a label _____ a jacket.
(f)   I took it _____ to the shop to complain.
(g)   'Is something wrong _____ it?' he said.
(h)   I asked _____ a refund.

Sport

Sports facilities and athletics

1   Put each of the following words or phrases in its correct place in the passage below.

officials	pools	courts	stadium	rink	field events
athletes	rings	pitches	scoreboard	spectators	track events

There's a big new sports centre near my home. There are football (a) _____, tennis and basketball (b) _____, swimming (c) _____, a sports hall with two boxing (d) _____ and even a skating (e) _____. There is also a separate athletics (f) _____, where 20,000 (g) _____ can watch the (h) _____ on the track and the (i) _____, such as jumping and throwing, in the grass centre. The (j) _____ get ready in modern changing rooms and the (k) _____ time and measure the events with modern equipment. A huge electronic (l) _____ shows the results.

Football

2   Instructions as above.

draw	track suits	captains	match	referee	amateurs
team	toss a coin	players	crowd	gymnasium	train

I play football for my local (a) _____ against other sides in the area. Of course the (b) _____ aren't paid, we're just (c) _____. But anyway we (d) _____ very hard in the evenings and we're lucky because we can use the (e) _____ of a local school. On the day of the (f) _____ we arrive early, change, and put on (g) _____ to keep warm. Then the (h) _____, dressed in black, calls the two (i) _____ to the centre to (j) _____ to decide who will play in which direction. Not many people come to watch the game. We usually have a (k) _____ of only one or two hundred. But we enjoy it, whether we win, lose or (l) _____.

3   Explain the difference between ...
(a)   amateurs and professionals
(b)   a winner and a runner-up
(c)   to win and to beat
(d)   a hurdle race and a relay race

4   Put one of the following words in each space in the sentences below.

on   for   of   at   in   between

(a)   Which team does he play _____?
(b)   She put _____ her tracksuit.
(c)   There's an exciting race taking place _____ the track.
(d)   I'm not very good _____ running.
(e)   She's the best player _____ the team.
(f)   There was a crowd _____ 50,000 _____ the stadium.
(g)   The result _____ the football match was a 2:2 draw.
(h)   The match was _____ Brazil and Argentina.
(i)   A runner-up comes second _____ a race or competition.

Television and Newspapers

Television

1   Put each of the following words or phrases in its correct place in the passage below.

viewers	subjective	mass media	quiz shows	indoctrinate
channels	objective	soap operas	commercials	switch

(a) _____ is a phrase often used to describe ways of giving information and entertainment to very large numbers of people. It includes newspapers, advertising and radio and, of course, television. In most countries people can (b) _____ to any of three or four different (c) _____. Do television programmes influence our minds? Do they (d) _____ us? Is the news completely (e) _____ (neutral) or is it (f) _____ (considered from one particular point of view)? Don't the (g) _____ for alcohol, food and other goods condition our minds? Even the (h) _____ going on week after week telling the story of one family or group of people sometimes make us want to copy the life-style we see on the screen. Also (i) _____ which give people big prizes for answering simple questions can make us greedy. Some programmes are watched by tens of millions of (j) _____.

Newspapers

2   Instructions as above.

cartoons	editorials	circulation	censorship	sensational
views	advertising	gossip columns	news agencies	
reviews	headlines	entertainment	correspondents	

A newspaper makes its money from the price people pay for it and also from the (a) _____ it carries. A popular newspaper with a (b) _____ of over five million daily makes a lot of money. Less serious newspapers are probably read just for (c) _____. They have big (d) _____ above the news stories, funny (e) _____ to look at and (f) _____ photos of violence. The (g) _____ are full of stories of the private lives of famous people. No one takes the political (h) _____ of such papers very seriously. On the other hand, in a free country where there is no (i) _____, serious newspapers are read principally for their news, sent to them by their (j) _____ round the world and by the big (k) _____. People also read these newspapers for their (l) _____ of new books, films and plays and for their (m) _____, which represent the opinion of the newspaper itself about the important events and issues of the moment.

3   Explain the difference between ...
(a)   viewers and listeners
(b)   mass circulation and small circulation
(c)   editor, reporter and critic

4   Put one of the following words in each of the sentences below.

in   on   for   to

(a)   This programme is boring. Switch _____ another channel.
(b)   It's a commercial _____ beer.
(c)   That actor's _____ a soap opera every Friday.
(d)   What's _____ television tonight?

Theatre

Parts of a theatre

1   Match each part of a theatre on the right with a definition on the left.

(a)   where actors put on their costumes and make-up   stalls
(b)   area on which the performance takes place   aisle
(c)   a line of seats   circle
(d)   a way down from back to front between the seats   dressing room
(e)   the area of downstairs seats   stage
(f)   the area of upstairs seats   box office
(g)   the theatre entrance hall where people meet before going in   row
(h)   the place where you go or phone to buy tickets   backstage
(i)   the whole area out of sight of the audience   box
(j)   a little private balcony with 3–5 seats only   foyer

Producing a play

2   Put each of the following words or phrases in its correct place in the passage below.

reviews	performances	audience	rehearsals	run	flop
director	theatre-goers	first night	auditions	hit	cast
critics	playwright	matinées	applause	parts	

The person who directs the preparation of a play is the (a) _____. Sometimes the (b) _____, who wrote the play, works with him. One of the first things to be done is to choose the (c) _____, the actors and actresses. For this purpose, (d) _____ are held at which actors perform short pieces and the most suitable are chosen for the (e) _____ in the play. Before the play is performed in front of an (f) _____ of hundreds of (g) _____, of course there are a lot of (h) _____. At last, the (i) _____! When the curtain goes down at the end, will there be enthusiastic (j) _____ or silence? Will the newspaper (k) _____ be good or bad? What will the (l) _____ think? Everyone hopes for a (m) _____ that will (n) _____ for months or even years, but the play might be a (o) _____ and only last a few days. It's hard work in the theatre. There are evening (p) _____ six nights a week and afternoon shows, called (q) _____, once or twice as well.

3   Put one of the following words in each of the spaces below.

to   in   behind   during   at   on

(a)   We sat _____ the stalls.
(b)   The usherette showed us _____ our seats.
(c)   There were two actors _____ the stage.
(d)   You'd better ask _____ the box office.
(e)   My favourite actress was _____ the play.
(f)   During the performance, work is going on _____ the scenes.
(g)   People usually have a drink or a cigarette _____ the interval.
(h)   Our seats were _____ the third row.
(i)   He prefers to sit _____ the front; she likes to be _____ the back.
(j)   I like to sit _____ the middle.

Travel

Holidays

1   Put each of the following words or phrases in its correct place in the passage below.

off the beaten track   **hitch-hiking**   **leisure**   **off-peak**
package holiday   **travel agents**   **resort**   **peak**
cut-price tickets   **youth hostels**

People have more money and more (a) _____ nowadays and even young people can afford to go abroad. Many (b) _____ offer cheap (c) _____ for flights to all parts of the world, so youngsters can avoid the crowded, well-known places and get to less famous areas which are (d) _____. Instead of using public transport and hotels, they can travel by (e) _____ and stay at (f) _____. But most people prefer some kind of (g) _____ at a popular holiday (h) _____, which means that everything is arranged for you and the price you pay includes transport, food and accommodation. Try to avoid taking your holiday during the busy (i) _____ tourist season. It's more crowded and expensive. If possible, go in the quieter (j) _____ period.

Journeys

2   Put each of the following words in its correct place in the passage below. Some words must be used more than once.

trip   travel   journey   cruise   tour   voyage   flight

(a)   For general advice about _____, go to a travel agent.
(b)   One day I would like to do the _____ by train and ship across Russia to Japan.
(c)   We're going on a _____ of Europe, visiting 11 countries in five weeks.
(d)   We went on a three-week _____ round the Mediterranean. The ship called at Venice, Athens, Istanbul and Alexandria.
(e)   He once went by ship to Australia. The _____ took 3½ weeks.
(f)   I'm going on a business _____ to Paris next weekend.
(g)   Air France _____ 507 from Paris to New York will be taking off in ten minutes.
(h)   The _____ from Heathrow Airport to the centre of London takes about 45 minutes by underground.
(i)   On our first day in New York we went on a three-hour _____ of the city by bus, which showed us the main sights.
(j)   During our stay in Paris we went on a day _____ to Disneyland.

3   Explain the difference between ...
(a)   a hotel and a bed and breakfast place
(b)   seasick, airsick and carsick
(c)   tour operator and travel agent
(d)   at sea and at the seaside

4   Put one of the following words in each space in the sentences below.

in   at   by   on

(a)   We went _____ car.
(b)   We went _____ John's car.
(c)   We went _____ a journey.
(d)   She arrived _____ Rome at midnight.
(e)   She arrived _____ the hotel.

War

The outbreak of war

1 Put each of the following words or phrases in its correct place in the passage below.

deteriorate	mobilise	hostile acts	declare war	clashes
aggression	outbreak	forces	ultimatum	retaliate

For years there were border (a) _____ between troops of country X and those of country Z. Then (b) _____ from X attacked a village in Z. Z accused X of (c) _____ and began to (d) _____ in readiness for possible war. X warned Z: 'If you carry out (e) _____ against us, we will (f) _____.' But there was more fighting on the border. The situation had begun to (g) _____. X delivered an (h) _____ to Z. 'If you do not promise to respect our borders, we will (i) _____. Finally came the (j) _____ of war.

Peace making

2 Instructions as above.

withdraw	intermediary	targets	neutral	peace treaty
get involved	intervene	ceasefire	civilian	peace-keeping force

After months of fighting, during which (a) _____ as well as military (b) _____ were bombed, country X asked country Y, which had remained (c) _____ during the hostilities, to act as an (d) _____, but Y decided not to (e) _____. X then asked the United Nations to (f) _____. The United Nations managed to arrange a (g) _____ and stationed a multi-national (h) _____ between the two opposing armies. After weeks of talks, the two countries finally signed a (i) _____ and the UN troops were able to (j) _____.

3 Explain the difference between ...
(a) to advance and to retreat
(b) war and civil war
(c) conventional war and nuclear war
(d) an ally and an enemy

4 Put one of the following words in each space in the sentences below.

as   on   in   for   out   between

(a) X declared war _____ Z.
(b) Troops are moving _____ readiness _____ an attack.
(c) Y didn't want to get involved _____ the fighting.
(d) The Second World War broke _____ in 1939.
(e) Canada acted _____ an intermediary _____ the argument.
(f) War planes carried _____ an attack.
(g) The peace-keeping force remained _____ the two enemy armies during peace talks, then withdrew.

Welfare State

1   Put each of the following words or phrases in its correct place in the passage below.

elderly	medical treatment	physically disabled	pension
schooling	eligible	out of work	social services
benefits	social workers	welfare state	retire
subsidised	low incomes	mentally handicapped	

A country which helps its old, sick, disabled and unemployed is called a (a) _____. (b) _____ people receive a state (c) _____ when they (d) _____ at the age of 60 or 65. People with (e) _____ who cannot afford to buy or rent decent accommodation are given houses or flats with (f) _____ rents, which means that the government or local council supports the rent to keep it low. Sick people get free (g) _____ from their doctor or at the hospital. Mothers of small children get special state financial (h) _____, and of course older children receive free (i) _____. (j) _____ people, who cannot move normally, and (k) _____ people, whose minds are not fully developed, also receive special assistance and, if necessary, special equipment to help them live normal lives. People who are (l) _____ are normally (m) _____ to receive unemployment benefit, which is paid by the state. The (n) _____ (government departments responsible for people's well-being) will help people who financially, physically or psychologically, have difficulty in coping with life and (o) _____ will visit such people in their homes.

2   Explain the difference between …
(a)   advice and advise
(b)   blind and deaf
(c)   free and subsidised
(d)   a hearing aid and braille
(e)   haves and have-nots

3   Put one of the following words in each space in the sentences below.

for   of   at   with   out   in

(a)   Disabled people sometimes find it difficult to cope _____ public transport.
(b)   He's been _____ _____ work for over a year.
(c)   _____ a welfare state, the government is responsible _____ people's well-being.
(d)   Social workers visited her _____ her home.
(e)   He retired _____ the age _____ 65.
(f)   After his accident, he received a disability pension _____ the rest of his life.

Work

Applying for a job

1   Put each of the following words or phrases in its correct place in the passage below.

references   short-list   experience   vacancy   qualifications
fill in   interview   applicants   apply   application forms

In times of high unemployment there are usually very many (a) _____ when a
(b) _____ is advertised. Sometimes large numbers of people (c) _____, and send
off (d) _____ for a single job. It is not unusual, in fact, for hundreds of people to
(e) _____ to a firm for one post. This number is reduced to a (f) _____ of
perhaps six or eight, from whom a final choice is made when they all attend an
(g) _____. Very possibly the people interviewing will be interested in the
(h) _____ the candidates gained at school or university and what (i) _____ they
have had in previous jobs. They will probably ask for (j) _____ written by the
candidates' teachers and employers.

Choosing the right job

2   Instructions as above.

commute   salary   prospects   promotion   retire
pension   ambitious   perks   increments   commission

Job satisfaction is important but I have a wife and baby so I have to think about
money too. If a job interests me, I need to know what (a) _____ it offers and also
whether there are regular annual increases, called (b) _____. I want to know if I
will receive a (c) _____ when I (d) _____ at the age of 60 or 65. If the job is
selling a product, I ask if I'll receive a percentage of the value of what I sell, called
(e) _____. It is also important to know if there are extra advantages, like free
meals or transport, or the free use of a car. These are called (f) _____ or fringe
benefits. Are the future (g) _____ good? For example, is there a good chance of
(h) _____ to a better job, with more money and responsibility? Is the job near my
home? If it isn't, I'll have to (i) _____ every day and this can be expensive. I am
very keen to be successful. I am very (j) _____. I don't want to stay in the same job
all my life.

3   Put one of the following words in each space in the sentences below.

at   in   for   to   as   off   of

(a)   I'm interested _____ this job.
(b)   What did you study _____ university?
(c)   He has applied _____ Lufthansa _____ a job _____ an office manager.
(d)   This job advertisement looks interesting. I'll send _____ an application form.
(e)   Have you filled _____ the form yet?
(f)   You must send _____ the form by 20 May.
(g)   He's been _____ that job for two years.
(h)   She retired _____ the age of 60.
(i)   A commission means you get a percentage _____ what you sell.
(j)   The use _____ a company car is a nice perk to have.
(k)   The sixty applicants were reduced _____ a short-list of four.

Mini Topics

Argument

Put each of the following words in its correct place in the passage below.

disagreement   friction   nag   resentment
aggressive   jealous   row   troublemaker

I've always had a feeling of (a) _____ towards my older brother, John, because he always received more attention from our parents. There has always been (b) _____ between us. And now that I'm more successful than he is in my job, he is (c) _____ of me. We've never actually had a (d) _____, just the occasional (e) _____, but we've never got on well. And his wife likes to make things worse. She's a real (f) _____, a nasty, argumentative, quarrelsome, (g) _____ woman. I've heard her (h) _____ John continually to get a better job, a bigger house, a nicer car.

Sadness

Instructions as above.

sob   heartbroken   tears   grief   recover
loss   withdrawn   miss   comfort   sleepless

When Susan's cat was killed by a car she burst into (a) _____ and began to (b) _____ so loudly that the neighbours next door heard her. She was (c) _____ by the (d) _____. Her mother tried to (e) _____ her but Susan's (f) _____ was so great that it was three days (and three (g) _____ nights) before she began to (h) _____ enough to eat normally. Even then she talked to no one and was silent and (i) _____ for weeks. I think she'll always (j) _____ her pet.

Nervousness

Instructions as above.

blush   sweat   tongue-tied   embarrassment   shy
nerves   stammer   tremble   tranquillizer   faint

I have to tell you that my (a) _____ aren't very good. Last week I went for a job interview and my hands began to (b) _____, my palms started to (c) _____ and my face was red because I always (d) _____ with (e) _____ on these occasions. I've always been very (f) _____ with other people. When I was asked questions I was completely (g) _____ and I could only (h) _____. I felt (i) _____ and wished I had a (j) _____ to calm me down. I didn't get the job. A pity. I would like to have been a television newsreader.

Success

Put each of the following words in its correct place in the passage below.

achieve	confidence	ladder	ambitious	exploit
achievement	determined	power	ruthless	ability

I've never been a (a) _____ in the normal sense. I've never wanted to be a manager or director. I've never wanted to reach the top of the (b) _____ or to have (c) _____. But I've always had a wish to (d) _____ something, to write a book, climb a mountain, win a prize. This is not because I want fame or money but just that simple feeling of (e) _____ you get when you've done something difficult. I'm not very sure of myself and it would be good for my (f) _____ to succeed in something. Some people will lie, (g) _____ other people, be dishonest, do anything, in order to succeed. They will be absolutely (h) _____. But I think the people who deserve to succeed are those who are (i) _____ and have (j) _____.

Fame

Put each of the following words or phrases in its correct place in the passage below.

interviews	bodyguards	break-up	privacy
in the public eye	autographs	celebrity	pressures
entourage	fans		

Being famous, being a (a) _____ can mean wealth, recognition and being surrounded by an (b) _____ of helpers, secretaries and agents. It can mean giving (c) _____ to admiring (d) _____ and (e) _____ to the press. But being (f) _____ also has its disadvantages. Famous entertainers suffer from a lack of (g) _____. They need (h) _____ to protect them. The constant (i) _____ on them can lead to the (j) _____ of their marriages. This is the price of fame.

Pride

Instructions as above.

boast	proud	vain	thick-skinned
conceited	pride	snob	contemptuous

Mrs Watson next door thinks she is better than other people. She thinks she is superior, 'high class'. In other words, she's a (a) _____. She is very (b) _____ of herself and very (c) _____ of other, 'ordinary' people. I've heard her (d) _____ to neighbours about her lovely house, her big car, her husband's high salary. She's a very (e) _____ person too, always admiring herself in a mirror. Mr Watson also has a very high opinion of himself. His neighbours think that he is a very (f) _____ person, but the Watsons are both so (g) _____ that other people's criticism of them has no effect on them at all. I think that one day they'll find that they have no friends left, and then they'll be sorry. (h) _____ comes before a fall.

Birth

Put each of the following words or phrases in its correct place in the passage below.

pregnant   **born**   **maternity ward**   **midwife**   **prams**   **cots**
deliver   **call**   **expecting**   **parents**   **crawl**

When a woman is (a) _____ a baby, we say that she is (b) _____. Babies are (c) _____ either at home or in the (d) _____ of a hospital. It is the job of a doctor or a (e) _____ to (f) _____ new babies. The proud (g) _____ must soon decide what to (h) _____ the child. For the first six months of their lives most babies are taken out in (i) _____ and sleep in (j) _____. At eight months or so they learn to (k) _____ along the floor, and they can usually walk soon after their first birthday.

Childhood and Adolescence

Put each of the following words in its correct place in the passage below.

hobbies   **development**   **extroverts**   **adult**   **relationships**
daydreams   **adults**   **introverts**   **idolise**   **teens**

Children live in their own world, from which (a) _____ are largely excluded. The (b) _____ world is strange and exciting to them. They have (c) _____ of success, adventure, romance and fame. They (d) _____ their big brothers and sisters, pop singers or film stars. (e) _____ such as stamp-collecting, music or dancing are important to them. Children, especially when they are in their (f) _____, go through a physical and emotional (g) _____ which can be frightening. Their characters also begin to develop. Some adolescents are (h) _____ and keep themselves to themselves, while others are (i) _____ and like to share their thoughts and form (j) _____ with other people. It's a wonderful, terrible time.

Death

Instructions as above.

mourners   **crematorium**   **dead**   **funeral**   **widow**   **will**
cemetery   **priest**   **leave**   **inherits**   **hearse**

The body of a person who has died is taken in a special car called a (a) _____ to the (b) _____ service, which is conducted by a (c) _____. The relatives and friends of the (d) _____ person, who are called the (e) _____, are there. Then the wooden coffin is buried in a grave in the (f) _____ or cremated in a (g) _____. When people get older they usually make a (h) _____ and (i) _____ their money and other things to their family and friends. When a man dies, it is usually his (j) _____ who (k) _____ his property.

Advertising

Put each of the following words or phrases in its correct place in the passage.

hoardings	classified advertisements	publicise	commercials
posters	advertising agencies	persuade	eye-catching

Advertisements are everywhere, from columns of small (a) _____ for houses, jobs, cars etc. in newspapers to big (b) _____ on walls and enormous advertisements on (c) _____ by the side of the road. The job of the (d) _____ is to (e) _____ the products of the firms who employ them. They design (f) _____ advertisements and make television (g) _____ to (h) _____ us to buy, buy, buy.

Art

Put each of the following words in its correct place in the passage below.

galleries	works	dealers	professional	sculptor
creative	sculpture	painter	amateur	reproductions

One of the most (a) _____ things anyone can do is to make a work of art, whether it's a (b) _____ making a (c) _____ or a (d) _____ painting pictures. (e) _____ artists do it for their own satisfaction and pleasure, but (f) _____ artists have to make a living from their art and they are dependent on (g) _____ to sell their (h) _____ in city (i) _____. I myself have three Picassos, a Botticelli and a Van Gogh. They're (j) _____, not originals, but they're all I can afford.

Photography

Instructions as above.

prints	album	enlargements	snaps
slides	camera	projector	develop

A lot of people buy a (a) _____ just to take holiday (b) _____. They have (c) _____ made and put them in an (d) _____ or sometimes they prefer (e) _____, which they can show on the wall or screen with a (f) _____. Other people are more serious. They (g) _____ and print their films themselves in their own darkroom at home. If they want big pictures they make (h) _____.

Military Service

Put each of the following words or phrases in its correct place in the passage below.

army	compulsory	forces	volunteers
navy	promotion	officer	air force

In some countries military service is (a) _____. All young men and sometimes young women must spend a year or two in the (b) _____. (In most countries nowadays they don't have to. All members of the armed services are (c) _____.) To be a soldier you join the (d) _____, to be a sailor you join the (e) _____ and to be an airman you join the (f) _____. If you are good at your job and can take responsibility, you might get (g) _____ and become an (h) _____.

Police

Instructions as above.

walkie-talkie **join**   **plain clothes** **detective**
police force   **rank**   **policeman**   **uniform**

Alan is now old enough and tall enough to (a) _____ the (b) _____. At first, of course, he'll be an ordinary (c) _____ of the lowest (d) _____. He'll wear a (e) _____ and go out in the streets keeping in touch with the police station with his (f) _____. Then he'd like to be a (g) _____ in (h) _____ investigating serious crime.

Security Work

Instructions as above.

guards   **tap**   **bullet-proof**   **armoured vehicles**   **bug**
kidnappers **couriers** **security firm**   **private detectives**

I run a (a) _____ which offers a complete range of security services. We have (b) _____ with special (c) _____ windows to transport money and other valuable items. We can supply trained (d) _____ to protect exhibits at art shows and jewellery displays. We can advise you if you think someone is trying to (e) _____ your phone or (f) _____ your private conversations at home or in the office with hidden microphones. We have ex-policemen whom you can hire as (g) _____ and special (h) _____ to deliver your valuable parcels anywhere in the world. We can protect you or your children against possible (i) _____.

The Countryside

Put each of the following words or phrases in its correct place in the passage below.

farms **unpolluted**   **relaxed**   **rural**   **wildlife**
pace   **national parks** **cultivated** **remote**   **villages**

Away from the urban problems of the city lies the (a) _____ peace and quiet of the countryside. The air is more likely to be clear and (b) _____, the (c) _____ of life is slower, and the people living in small (d) _____ more (e) _____ and friendly. Some land is (f) _____ and you'll see crops growing, as well as animals grazing, on the (g) _____. Some areas of particular natural beauty are designated as (h) _____ by the government, and here (i) _____ can live and move about safely. It is in places (j) _____ from the noisy cities that you can experience the true beauty of nature.

STREET ENGLISH

Native speakers do not always speak the kind of careful, clear English that you might expect. Someone who says, 'wozzat?' means 'What's that?' A sound like 'kew' means 'thank you'. What would you understand from these?

'dunno   **'assokay**   **'wotcher'dooin?**   **'eeryiz**   **'oozat?**

The Seaside

Put each of the following words in its correct place in the passage below.

lifeguards	depth	waves	shallow	horizon
beach	drown	dive	currents	cliffs

Many people's idea of relaxation is to sit on a sandy (a) _____ gazing at the broad (b) _____ or watching the (c) _____ roll in one after the other. But the sea can be dangerous and every year hundreds of bathers (d) _____ either when they are carried out to sea by strong (e) _____ or simply because they can't swim and find themselves out of their (f) _____ with their feet no longer touching the bottom. And hundreds more have to be rescued by (g) _____. If you want to (h) _____ into the sea, from rocks or some other high point, make sure it's deep enough. If it's (i) _____, you could seriously injure yourself. And finally, if you decide to walk along the high (j) _____ overlooking the beach and the sea, don't go too near the edge.

Mountains

Instructions as above.

mountaineers	ropes	oxygen	ascent	peak
equipment	range	height	descent	climb

The Himalayas are the best-known mountain (a) _____ in the world and Mt Everest, with a (b) _____ of 8,880 metres is the highest mountain. Since Edmund Hillary made the first (c) _____ in 1953, (d) _____ from many countries have managed to (e) _____ to the (f) _____. Normally they need to take (g) _____ cylinders to help them breathe and other special (h) _____, including (i) _____ to connect themselves to each other. It's a dangerous sport and many people have lost their lives, not just on the way up but during the (j) _____ as well.

Electrical Appliances

Put each of the following words in its correct place in the passage below.

electrician	adjust	switch	lead	controls
dealer	plug	knob	socket	unplug

When you buy a television, radio or cassette recorder make sure it has a long enough (a) _____. (b) _____ it in at the most convenient (c) _____ in your room, and then (d) _____ on. You normally (e) _____ the volume by turning a (f) _____, and there are other (g) _____ as well. It is probably best to (h) _____ the appliance when it is not in use. If you have any trouble with it, ask an (i) _____ to look at it or take it back to the (j) _____ you bought it from.

The Telephone

Put each of the following words or phrases in its correct place in the passage below.

receiver	line	look up	engaged
dial	directory	get through	operator

How easy it is to use the telephone! Nowadays we usually don't need the (a) _____ to connect us to friends in other countries. We can (b) _____ the number in the telephone (c) _____, pick up the (d) _____ and (e) _____ the number. If the number is not (f) _____, we (g) _____ straightaway and if it's a good (h) _____, we can have a clear, easy conversation with people on the other side of the world.

Computers

Instructions as above.

software	computers	screen	word processor
hardware	calculator	keyboard	printer

So you only have a pocket (a) _____ to do additions, multiplications and so on, and you want to know about real (b) _____? Right. Well, the machines themselves are called the (c) _____ and the programs that you feed into them are called the (d) _____. If you want to see the results of what you are doing, you'll need a (e) _____ or you'll have to plug in to a television set. You'll operate your machine like a typewriter by pressing keys on the (f) _____. If you want a record on paper of what you're doing, you'll need a (g) _____, and if you want a machine which will enable you to see, arrange, re-arrange and then print a page of material, then the machine you want is a (h) _____. You want colour? Well, you can …

Factory Work

Put each of the following words or phrases in its correct place in the passage below.

labour relations	tea break	apprentice	factory	canteen
management	foreman	white collar	shop floor	manual

I like to work with my hands; in other words, I like (a) _____ work. I have never wanted to be a (b) _____ worker, as I would be bored with office work. So I have been taken on as an (c) _____ in a (d) _____ for two years to learn to be a machine-operator. I work with a group of men under a (e) _____, who tells us what to do, when we can go to the (f) _____ for lunch or take a (g) _____ and so on. (h) _____ are quite good and the (i) _____ spend a lot of time on the (j) _____ mixing with the workers. I've got no complaints.

Office Work

Instructions as above.

typewriter	callers	stationery	dictate
shorthand	correspondence	filing cabinets	file

I do general work in a small office. I deal with all (a) _____ coming into and sent from the office and (b) _____ these letters alphabetically in big metal (c) _____ near my desk. I answer the telephone and give (d)_____ the information they want. If the manager wants to (e) _____ a letter, I take it down in (f) _____ on my pad and type it on my electric (g) _____. Of course it's important that we always have enough paper and envelopes and so on, and it's one of my jobs to buy this (h) _____ when we need it. I don't know what they'd do without me!

A Strike

Instructions as above.

unemployment	dispute	go on strike	dismiss	deadlock
shop steward	on the dole	redundant	picket line

1,600 workers at the Ace Cycle Factory decided to (a) _____ last week following a (b) _____ with the management, who last month decided to (c) _____ two men for unsatisfactory work. The men complained to their (d) _____, who told the union. The management and the union have had talks but these soon ended in (e) _____. The area in which the factory is situated is already an area of high (f) _____, with one adult in five (g) _____ (out of work and receiving state aid). The striking workers have formed a (h) _____ outside the factory gates to prevent other workers from going in to work. The management say that 20% of the workers will have to be made (i) _____ next year anyway because of the decreased demand for cycles.

POLITICALLY CORRECT ENGLISH

Nowadays people are very sensitive not to offend women, poor people, the old and various minority groups. The careful language used to refer to such people is called, ironically, 'politically correct'. Here are some 'politically correct' expressions with their meaning in brackets.

non wage-earner (unemployed)
financially underprivileged (poor)
substance abuser (drug addict)
overseas visitor (foreign tourist)
vertically disadvantaged (short person)
personkind (mankind)
guest of the correctional system (prison convict)
she-ro (hero)

Related Word Groups

Sounds

1   Put each of the following words in its correct place in the sentences below.

rumble   whistle   crash   squeal   roar
creak   rustle   bang   clatter   splash

(a)   We heard a _____ of tyres. It was a police-car turning a corner at top speed.
(b)   The plates and glasses fell to the floor with a _____.
(c)   We live near the airport and there's a terrible _____ every time a plane goes overhead.
(d)   The day was very quiet and we could hear the _____ of leaves in the wind.
(e)   He fell into the water with a great _____.
(f)   I heard a _____. It sounded like a gun-shot.
(g)   It was an enormous, heavy, old, wooden door and it used to _____ loudly when anyone opened it.
(h)   It was the best football match I've ever seen. Both teams played hard until the final _____.
(i)   The metal tray fell down the stone stairs with a _____.
(j)   I could hear the _____ of thunder in the distance.

2   Instructions as above.

hum   peal   crack   tick   squeak   pop   pips   jingle

(a)   There was no sound except the quiet _____ of the air-conditioning.
(b)   At every hour on the radio there are six _____ so that people can check the precise time.
(c)   The champagne cork finally came out with a loud _____.
(d)   Be careful. The ice is very thin and I think I heard it _____.
(e)   To celebrate the happy event, all the church bells in the town began to _____.
(f)   I must oil my bike. There's a _____ somewhere in the back wheel.
(g)   The engine of a Rolls Royce is so quiet that even when the car is going fast you can hear the clock _____.
(h)   The animals had small bells round their necks, which used to _____ when they moved.

TONGUE-TWISTERS

A tongue-twister is a phrase which is very difficult to pronounce. Say each of the following repeatedly as quickly as you can.

Good blood, bad blood.
Peter Piper picked a peck of pickled pepper.
Sharon sells sea-shells on the sea-shore.

Animal Sounds

Match each animal with the sound it makes.

(a)	monkey	roar		(j)	sheep	bleat
(b)	lion	cluck		(k)	elephant	bray
(c)	dog	miaow, purr		(l)	pig	hiss
(d)	cat	chatter		(m)	donkey	trumpet
(e)	horse	crow		(n)	frog	grunt, squeal
(f)	hen	bark, growl		(o)	snake	squeak
(g)	cock	moo		(p)	duck	howl
(h)	bee	neigh		(q)	wolf	quack
(i)	cow	buzz		(r)	mouse	croak

Human Sounds

Put each of the following verbs in its correct place in the sentences below.

sniff   **cough**   **puff**   **yawn**   **hiccup**   **stammer**
snore   **sigh**   **pant**   **whisper** **sneeze**   **groan**

(a) He was so nervous he could only _____, 'I ...I ... I ... I'm pleased to meet you.'

(b) Don't _____ all the time. Use a handkerchief and blow your nose.

(c) If we are out of breath after running we _____ and _____.

(d) It is said that people _____ if they sleep with their mouths open and on their backs.

(e) He drank a lot of beer quickly and began to _____.

(f) If you have a cold and you _____, we often say, 'Bless you'.

(g) Don't speak so loud! Just _____. The children are asleep.

(h) I always used to _____ in history lessons. They were so boring.

(i) He can't stop talking. We always _____ with relief when he goes away.

(j) Smoking always makes me _____.

(k) My children _____ when I tell them they must go to bed.

METAPHORS AND SIMILES

We use these figures of speech not only in literary language but also in everyday speech. A metaphor is when we describe something as something else and we do not expect our words to be taken literally. e.g. 'He has a **heart of stone**'. (His heart isn't really made of stone).

I'll make you eat your words.   **He's a monster.**
I'm dying for a cigarette.   **It was a real nightmare.**

A simile is when we **compare** two things.

He's as strong as a bull.   **She can run like the wind.**
This room is like a pig-sty.   **It was as hot as hell.**

Ways of Looking

Put each of the following verbs in its correct place in the sentences below.

frown	**stare**	**peep**	**wink**	**glance**
peer	**glare**	**gaze**	**glimpse**	**blink**

(a)   That man does look rather strange but you shouldn't _____ at him.

(b)   He made a hole in the fence so that he could _____ through without being seen.

(c)   If you go out into bright sunlight after being in the dark, you sometimes _____.

(d)   Small boys often stand outside the bicycle shop and _____ at the wonderful machines in the window.

(e)   We _____ if we are rather annoyed or if we are concentrating.

(f)   Did you _____ someone pass the window a moment ago? I thought I just saw someone.

(g)   I thought he was serious until I saw him _____ at me to show he was joking.

(h)   Grandfather has very bad eyes. He has to _____ at the newspaper to read it.

(i)   I saw the motorist get out of his car and _____ furiously at the other driver who had run into the back of him.

(j)   I saw him _____ quickly at his watch.

Walking

Put each of the following verbs in its correct place in the sentences below.

stray	**wander**	**crawl**	**trip**	**dash**	**trudge**
creep	**stagger**	**limp**	**stroll**	**march**	**slip**

(a)   He was completely drunk. I watched him _____ across the road and fall down.

(b)   It's very pleasant for a tourist to _____ round a new city with no particular purpose or destination.

(c)   It was a lovely day so we decided to _____ in the park for an hour.

(d)   His injured foot made him _____ badly.

(e)   Be careful or you'll _____ on this icy bit of pavement.

(f)   Everyone was asleep when I returned so I had to _____ to my room without making a noise.

(g)   If you join the army, you'll have to learn to _____.

(h)   Please don't _____ away from the main group or you'll get lost.

(i)   Before babies can walk, they can only _____ on their hands and knees.

(j)   I'm afraid someone will _____ over that piece of wood and fall.

(k)   It began to rain and we had to _____ into a shop to keep dry.

(l)   The exhausted men had to _____ for five miles through the snow.

Body Movements

1 Match each item on the left with the most suitable phrase on the right.
(a)	He flexed	his head in disagreement.
(b)	He shook	his fists angrily.
(c)	He clenched	his neck to see better.
(d)	He craned	his muscles proudly.
(e)	He snapped	his forehead with a handkerchief.
(f)	He shrugged	his foot in time to the music.
(g)	He wiped	his shoulders.
(h)	He folded	his breath under water.
(i)	He scratched	his knee because it was painful.
(j)	He held	his arms and relaxed.
(k)	He tapped	his head thoughtfully.
(l)	He rubbed	his fingers to get attention.

2 Instructions as above.
(a)	He trembled	in the hot sun.
(b)	He shivered	with embarrassment.
(c)	he sweated	with fear.
(d)	He blushed	when he heard the sad news.
(e)	He sobbed	with cold.
(f)	He started	after going without food for three days.
(g)	He dozed	in surprise at the sudden noise.
(h)	He fainted	in his armchair after a hard day's work.

3 Instructions as above.
(a)	She nodded	when she saw her friend getting off the bus.
(b)	He bowed	when his commanding officer entered the room.
(c)	She curtseyed	in agreement.
(d)	She waved	when she was introduced to the Queen.
(e)	He smiled	when he was introduced to the Queen.
(f)	He saluted	to show the shop assistant what he wanted.
(g)	She fidgeted	because he was happy.
(h)	He pointed	after sitting in the same position for so long.

TOWNS IN IDIOMS

Newcastle is the centre of a major coal-producing area. To **send coals to Newcastle** is to give someone something he already has.

After a successful military campaign throughout Europe, Napoleon was finally defeated at Waterloo. If you **meet your Waterloo**, you come to a similar fate.

If someone asks you to do a very difficult job very quickly, you can reply, **'Rome wasn't built in a day'**.

If people ignore or avoid an unpopular person, we say that they **send him to Coventry**.

4   Put each of the following verbs in its correct place in the sentences below.

punch   **grab**   **stretch**   **stroke**   **slap**
squeeze   **grope**   **nudge**   **beckon**   **pat**

(a)   After driving his taxi all day, Teddy likes to get out and _____ his arms and legs

(b)   Some parents _____ their naughty children.

(c)   If he says that to me again, I'll _____ him on the nose.

(d)   When I was small, my father used to _____ me on the head when he was pleased with me.

(e)   She loved cats, and always used to stop and _____ any cats she saw.

(f)   Several people saw two men smash the shop window, _____ some diamonds, get into their car and drive away.

(g)   He was slim so he was just able to _____ between the two tables.

(h)   It was absolutely dark and I had to _____ in front of me to find the door.

(i)   My brother went to sleep during the church service and I had to _____ him with my elbow to wake him.

(j)   When it's your turn for a luggage check, the customs officer will _____ you to come forward.

Containers

Match each container on the left with its contents on the right.

(a)   basket   clothes and personal things for a long stay
(b)   trunk   coins
(c)   tank   bank notes, tickets
(d)   safe   shopping
(e)   vase   petrol, water
(f)   purse   suits, jackets, dresses
(g)   wallet   cash, secret documents, jewellery
(h)   kettle   boiling water
(i)   wardrobe   flowers
(j)   briefcase   school books
(k)   envelope   clothes and belongings for a week's holiday
(l)   jug   letter
(m) suitcase   water, milk
(n)   barrel   waste paper
(o)   satchel   beer
(p)   bin   hot tea, cold drinks
(q)   box   business papers
(r)   (thermos) flask   chocolates, matches

Furniture and Fittings

Match each item from the following list with the correct letter from the
pictures below.

chest of drawers	table	bed	bookcase	cushion	pillow
cupboard	chair	desk	carpet	wardrobe	stool
washbasin	sofa	rug	mattress	armchair	sheet
lampshade	shelf	lamp	curtains	blanket	drawer

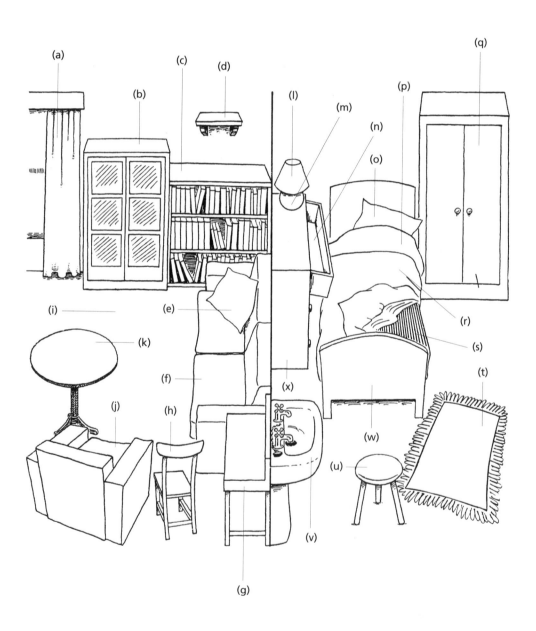

Connectors

1   Match each of the following connectors with the correct picture below.

nail	nut	pin	screw	bolt	safety pin	rubber band
rope	string	chain	thread	needle	drawing pin	paper clip

(a)

(b)

(c)

(d)

(e)

(f)

(g)

(h)

(i)

(j)

(k)

(l)

(m)

(n)

2   Complete each of the following sentences with the correct connector from the list above, making it plural if necessary.

(a)   We sew cloth with a _____ and _____.

(b)   We tie up a parcel with _____.

(c)   Mountaineers use _____ to keep together and avoid falling.

(d)   To keep a baby's nappy in place we use _____.

(e)   We use a hammer to knock a _____ into wood.

(f)   To pin a notice to a notice board we use a _____.

(g)   To keep pieces of cloth together in dressmaking we use _____.

(h)   We keep pieces of paper together firmly with a _____.

(i)   Different parts of a bicycle and other machines are kept together with _____ and _____.

(j)   We use a screwdriver to put in or take out _____.

(k)   Large ships in port are kept in place with heavy iron _____.

(l)   The postman keeps all the letters for one street together with a _____, made of elastic.

Tools

1 Match each of the following tools with the correct picture below.

spanner   hammer   axe   saw   screwdriver
spade   penknife   chisel   fork   drill
scissors   mallet   jack   rake

(a) (b) (c) (d) (e) (f) (g) (h) (i) (j) (k) (l) (m) (n)

2 Complete each of the following sentences with the correct tool from the list above.

(a) We cut paper or cloth with a pair of _____.
(b) We put in and take out screws with a _____.
(c) We dig holes in the ground with a _____.
(d) We make holes in wood, metal or stone with a _____.
(e) We raise a car to change a wheel with a _____.
(f) We knock nails into wood with a _____.
(g) We cut down trees with an _____.
(h) We carve wood or stone with a _____.
(i) We hit a chisel with a _____.
(j) We collect dry leaves and make earth level with a _____.
(k) To cut string and other things, we carry in our pocket a folding _____.
(l) We turn the earth over in the garden with a spade or _____.
(m) We saw wood with a _____.
(n) We tighten or loosen nuts and bolts with a _____.

Vehicles

Match each of the following vehicles with the correct picture below.

car	lorry	motorbike	ambulance	caravan	van
bus	tanker	bulldozer	trailer	scooter	coach

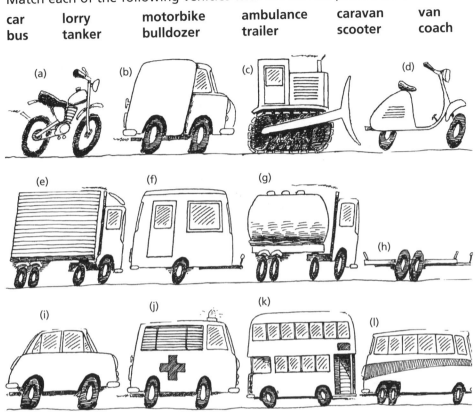

Bicycle

Match each of the following bicycle parts with the correct letter in the picture below.

saddle	frame	brakes	mudguard	back light
spokes	bell	pedal	handlebars	tyre
gears	chain	pump	front light	

Collective Nouns

Put each of the following collective nouns in its correct place in the sentences below, making it plural if necessary. Some nouns must be used more than once.

flock	herd	bundle	mob	stack	suite	congregation
shoal	bunch	crowd	fleet	crew	clump	audience
pack	set	swarm	gang	flight		

(a) The _____ of the British Royal Navy was very strong in the nineteenth century.
(b) Disease reduced the farmer's _____ from 90 to 65 cows.
(c) She was attacked by a _____ of wasps.
(d) A _____ of shouting people overturned cars, set fire to shops and attacked a police station.
(e) The Irish Prime Minister occupied a _____ of rooms at the hotel.
(f) Some spectators in the _____ disagreed with the referee's decision.
(g) He bought a large _____ of bananas.
(h) The priest was very sad to see his _____ getting smaller week by week.
(i) Fishing boats use modern equipment to locate the _____ of fish.
(j) She lost her balance and fell down a _____ of steps.
(k) He was the leader of a well-known _____ of criminals.
(l) We sat down in the shade of a _____ of trees.
(m) In spring _____ of birds arrive back in Europe after spending the winter in Africa.
(n) Our picnic was completely ruined by a _____ of ants.
(o) He gave her a _____ of flowers.
(p) British Airways has a _____ of 26 Boeing 747s.
(q) She gave a _____ of old clothes to a charity organisation.
(r) The _____ applauded the new play enthusiastically.
(s) Has anyone seen a _____ of keys? I left them somewhere.
(t) Golf is an expensive game. You'll need a _____ of clubs.
(u) The books were arranged in a _____ one on top of the other.
(v) They've bought a leather three-piece _____ – a sofa and two armchairs.
(w) Let's play a game. Who's got a _____ of cards?
(x) The cruise ship carries 150 passengers and a _____ of 85.
(y) The _____ of sheep was controlled by a shepherd and two dogs.
(z) For their wedding I gave them a _____ of cutlery (6 knives, 6 spoons, 6 forks etc.).

MISPRINTS

Misprints (printing errors) can produce amusing results.
Can you spot the misprints in these sentences?

He took some flowers to his ant in hospital.
She sent them a car every Christmas.
They had a Mercedes cat.
He cleans widows for a living.
Tomorrow will be bright with funny intervals.

Young Animals

For each animal below give the name of its young from the following list.

piglet   **kitten**   **cub**   **chick**   **lamb**
calf   **foal**   **duckling**   **puppy**   **kid**

(a) wolf
(b) horse
(c) pig
(d) fox
(e) dog
(f) cow

(g) cat
(h) lion
(i) duck
(j) sheep
(k) goat
(l) hen

Law Breakers

1   Match each person on the left with the correct definition on the right.

(a) an arsonist   attacks and robs people, often in the street
(b) a shoplifter   sets fire to property illegally
(c) a mugger   is anyone who breaks the law
(d) an offender   breaks into houses or other buildings to steal
(e) a vandal   steals from shops while acting as an ordinary customer
(f) a burglar   kills someone
(g) a murderer   deliberately causes damage to property
(h) a kidnapper   steals things from people's pockets in crowded places
(i) a pickpocket   gets secret information from another country
(j) an accomplice   buys and sells drugs illegally
(k) a drug dealer   takes away people by force, demanding money for their return
(l) a spy   helps a criminal in a criminal act
(m) a terrorist   uses violence for political reasons

2   Instructions as above.

(a) an assassin   causes damage or disturbance in public places
(b) a hooligan   hides on a ship or plane to get a free journey
(c) a stowaway   takes control of a plane by force & makes the pilot change course
(d) a thief   murders for political reasons or a reward
(e) a hijacker   is someone who steals
(f) a forger   makes counterfeit (false) money or signatures
(g) a robber   is a member of a criminal group
(h) a smuggler   steals money etc. by force from people or places
(i) a traitor   marries illegally, being married already
(j) a gangster   is a soldier who runs away from the army
(k) a deserter   brings goods into a country illegally without paying tax
(l) a bigamist   betrays his or her country to another state

Occupations

1 Match each person on the left with the correct definition on the right.

(a)	a traffic warden	arranges shop-window displays
(b)	a dustman	makes brick buildings and walls
(c)	a window dresser	works in a government ministry
(d)	an estate agent	controls parking and parking meters
(e)	a secretary	collects rubbish from people's houses
(f)	an undertaker	treats sick animals
(g)	a bricklayer	helps people buy and sell houses
(h)	a civil servant	sells newspapers and magazines from a shop
(i)	a vet	delivers babies
(j)	a newsagent	makes arrangements for funerals
(k)	a midwife	deals with office correspondence and records

2 Instructions as above.

(a)	a chef	drives someone's car for them
(b)	an architect	types letters in an office
(c)	a librarian	designs buildings
(d)	a fishmonger	operates on sick people
(e)	a miner	cooks in a restaurant or hotel
(f)	a curator	designs the insides of houses, hotels etc.
(g)	an interior decorator	runs a museum
(h)	a typist	works in a library
(i)	a chauffeur	gets coal from under the ground
(j)	a surgeon	sells fish from a shop

3 Instructions as above.

(a)	an optician	rides racehorses
(b)	a clown	loads and unloads ships in a port
(c)	a jockey	sells valuable objects at an auction
(d)	an auctioneer	makes people laugh at a circus
(e)	an editor	tests people's eyes and sells glasses
(f)	a docker	writes for a newspaper
(g)	a chiropodist	sells flowers from a shop
(h)	a butcher	represents his or her country at an embassy
(i)	a reporter	sells meat
(j)	a diplomat	prepares books, newspapers etc. for publication
(k)	a florist	treats people's feet

NON-WORDS

People in different parts of the world use different sounds (not words, just sounds) in different situations. In English-speaking countries people often say **'mmm'** when something tastes delicious, **'ouch!'** if they are hurt, **'wow!'** if they are impressed, **'ssh!'** if they want someone to be quiet and **'ah!'** if they suddenly see or understand something.

Male and Female

Complete each pair below by adding the male or female equivalent.

(a)	king	_____	(j)	_____	nun
(b)	husband	_____	(k)	waiter	_____
(c)	bridegroom	_____	(l)	_____	princess
(d)	_____	heroine	(m)	nephew	_____
(e)	boy scout	_____	(n)	_____	actress
(f)	_____	barmaid	(o)	host	_____
(g)	_____	policewoman	(p)	landlord	_____
(h)	air steward	_____	(q)	_____	widow
(i)	_____	headmistress	(r)	_____	aunt

People

The words below on the left are used in colloquial conversation to describe people of different characteristics or interests. Match each item on the left with the most suitable phrase on the right.

(a)	a chatterbox	is inquisitive and pokes his or her nose into other people's business
(b)	a highbrow	can't stop talking
(c)	a nosey parker	loves reading books
(d)	a bookworm	is confused and forgetful
(e)	a film fan	is intellectual and likes serious literature, art, music
(f)	a slowcoach	loves to work
(g)	a lazybones	is very keen on the cinema
(h)	a scatterbrain	is not very active or energetic
(i)	a workaholic	is slow
(j)	a fresh air fiend	causes difficulties between people
(k)	a high flier	seems to enjoy preventing others from enjoying themselves
(l)	a troublemaker	likes to open the windows or be outside
(m)	a killjoy	is clever and ambitious and will get promotion and success

---

WORD ORIGINS

English words come not only from Anglo-Saxon, Latin and French but also from a variety of more recent sources. Can you add to these examples?

People's names: Candido Jacuzzi, W. H. Hoover, Louis Braille, the Hooligan family

Combined words: camcorder, docu-drama, intercom, chocaholic, Eurocrat, hazchem

Acronyms: radar (radio detection and ranging), laser, aids, NASA, NATO

New inventions: walkman, velcro, bleeper, internet, CD Rom, microwave, hovercraft

Foreign ideas: karaoke (Japan), machismo (Spain), sauna (Finland), ombudsman (Sweden)

Clothes

1   Match each of the following items of clothing with the correct letter in the pictures below.

jacket	socks	boots	suit	apron	cap	overcoat
shorts	shirt	tee-shirt	pullover	trousers	shoes	waistcoat
sandals	tie	dress	skirt	slippers	scarf	blouse
pyjamas	hat					

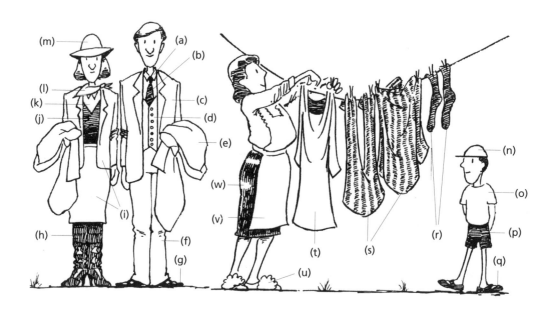

2   Match each of the following parts of clothing with the correct letter in the pictures below.

label	heel	collar	lapel	sole	seam	pocket
crease	sleeve	belt	laces	toe	lining	cuff
button	zip	buckle				

Wear/Dress

3   Put the correct form of wear or dress in the spaces below.

(a)   Students normally _____ very informally.
(b)   She often _____ in black.
(c)   They usually _____ jeans and sweaters.
(d)   They were _____ in jeans and sweaters.
(e)   What were they _____?
(f)   How were they _____?
(g)   He can wash, shave and _____ in ten minutes.
(h)   She was _____ an evening _____.
(i)   The men were in evening _____.
(j)   It's informal. There's no need to _____ up.

4   Put one of the following prepositions in each space in the sentences below.

on   in   off   up

(a)   Your jacket's undone. Button it _____.
(b)   It was very warm. We took _____ our coats.
(c)   Put _____ your pullover. It's cold.
(d)   That's the man, _____ the dark suit.
(e)   Hang your coat _____.
(f)   Hang your coat _____ the hook.
(g)   He took _____ his shoes and put _____ some slippers.
(h)   Anna's the girl _____ the red dress.
(i)   She's only three. She can't do her coat _____ by herself.
(j)   He rolled _____ his sleeves and started work.

PUNS 1

A pun is a humorous use of a word with two different meanings or two similar-sounding words with different meanings. Puns are often used in advertisements and newspaper headlines. They are also used in jokes like the following.

Where's that girl from?
Alaska.
It's O.K. I'll ask her myself.

Where do you go to weigh a whale?
A whale-weigh station.

My wife's gone to the Caribbean.
Jamaica?
No, she wanted to go.

Parts of the Body

1 Match each of the following parts of the head with the correct letter in the picture below.

hair   eyebrow   mouth   eye   eyelid   chin   lips   jaw
throat   forehead   nose   neck   eyelashes   nostril   cheek   ear

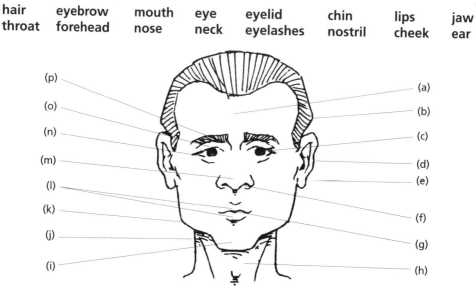

2 Match each of the following parts of the body with the correct letter in the picture below.

shoulder   calf   chest   thigh   leg   sole   palm   thumb
forearm   arm   shin   wrist   hand   waist   nail   elbow
stomach   toe   knee   ankle   heel   foot   hip   finger

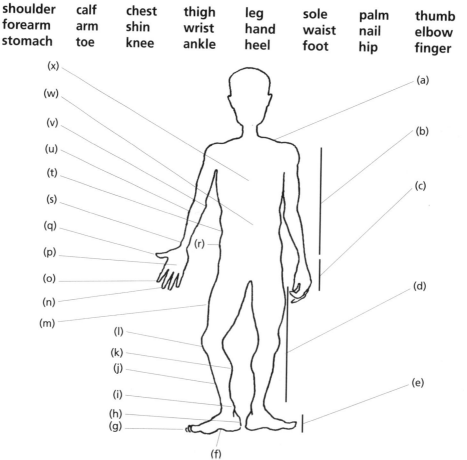

Punctuation Marks and Printing

Match each of the following items with the correct letter near the text below.

apostrophe   small letter   heading   dash   comma
capital letter   subheading   bracket   full stop   asterisk
inverted commas   underlining   stroke   colon   hyphen
question mark   semicolon   paragraph   footnote   italics
exclamation mark   abbreviation

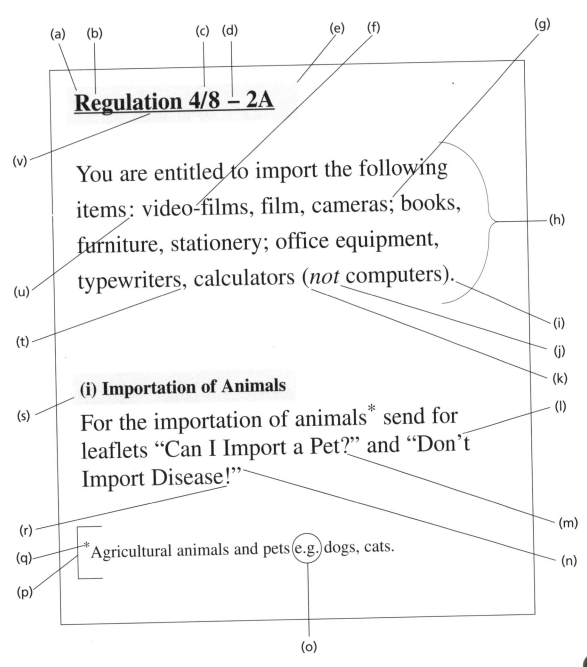

(a)   (b)   (c)   (d)   (e)   (f)   (g)

Regulation 4/8 – 2A

You are entitled to import the following items: video-films, film, cameras; books, furniture, stationery; office equipment, typewriters, calculators (*not* computers).

(i) Importation of Animals

For the importation of animals* send for leaflets "Can I Import a Pet?" and "Don't Import Disease!"

*Agricultural animals and pets (e.g.) dogs, cats.

(v) (u) (t) (s) (r) (q) (p) (h) (i) (j) (k) (l) (m) (n) (o)

55

British Measurements

Put each of the following words in its correct place in the sentences below.

ounce	gallon	inch	foot	yard
stone	pound	acre	mile	pint

(a) 1 _____ = 2.54 centimetres

(b) 1 _____ = 0.3048 metre

(c) 1 _____ = 0.9144 metre

(d) 1 _____ = 1,609.35 metres

(e) 1 _____ = 0.405 hectare

(f) 1 _____ = 28.35 grams

(g) 1 _____ = 0.454 kilogram

(h) 1 _____ = 6.35 kilograms

(i) 1 _____ = 0.568 litre

(j) 1 _____ = 4.55 litres

Quantities

We buy things in different units. Match each item on the left with the most suitable item on its right.

(a) a bar   of matches

(b) a pair   of soap

(c) a box   of potatoes

(d) a pound   of cloth

(e) a roll   of shoes

(f) an ounce   of milk

(g) a yard   of tobacco

(h) a pint   of film

(i) an acre   of flowers

(j) a bottle   of toothpaste

(k) a gallon   of land

(l) a bunch   of wine

(m) a tin   of sardines

(n) a tube   of petrol

(o) a packet   of jam

(p) a jar   of cigarettes

PUNS 2

Here are some puns in advertisements. Do you understand them?

WE'RE ALWAYS PLEASED TO MEAT YOU. (chain of butchers' shops)

REST ASSURED. (bed manufacturers)

YOUR VIEWS ARE REFLECTED IN THE MIRROR. (Mirror newspaper)

THE METEOROLOGISTS CAN'T GUARANTEE AN INDIAN SUMMER. BUT WE CAN. (Indian Tourist Office)

NEXT TIME YOU WANT TO BE AT YOUR BEST FOR A SPECIAL OCCASION, CONSIDER THE PRODUCTS OF THE AROMATA COMPANY (IT MAKES LOTS OF SCENTS). (perfume company)

Shapes

Put each of the following words in its correct place in the sentences below.

right angle	**lower**	**vertical**	**size**	**square**	**upper**
horizontal	**shape**	**triangle**	**angle**	**diagonal**	**centre**
rectangle	**circle**	**parallel**	**corner**		

These two diagrams are of the same
(a) _____ but of a different (b) _____.

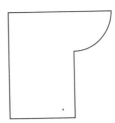

This is a (c) _____ with the (d) _____
lines twice as long as the (e) _____ ones.

This is a (f) _____ with a (g) _____ line
going from the (h) _____ to the top
left-hand (i) _____.

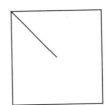

This is a (j) _____. Each bottom (k) _____
is 45°. The top one is a (l) _____ (90°).

These two lines are (m) _____ to each other.
The (n) _____ line is longer than the
(o) _____ one. There is a (p) _____
between them.

Britain and the British Isles

Britain consists of England, Scotland and Wales. The United Kingdom consists of Britain and Northern Ireland. Match each item below with the correct number on the map.

Countries/Regions (1-10)

CORNWALL: beautiful SW county, adjective/language: Cornish
EAST ANGLIA: flat area in E. England, counties: Suffolk, Norfolk
ENGLAND: pop 46 mill. (of 56 mill. in UK)
HOME COUNTIES: round London, especially Surrey, Essex, Kent
REPUBLIC OF IRELAND: 'Eire', pop. 3 mill., 94% Catholic
MIDLANDS: central area of England
NORTHERN IRELAND: 'Ulster', in UK but not Britain
SCOTLAND: in UK but with separate educational and legal systems
WALES: coal/industry in S, mountains in N, Welsh still spoken
WEST COUNTRY: SW counties of England

Sea Areas (11-14)

CHANNEL: world's busiest waterway, new tunnel to France
IRISH SEA: between Britain & Ireland
NORTH SEA: E. of Britain, undersea gas & oil
BRISTOL CHANNEL: between S. Wales & England

Towns/Cities (15-35)

BATH: West Country town, stone buildings, Roman baths
BELFAST: port, industry, capital of Northern Ireland
BRISTOL: port in West Country, industry, NW of Bath
BIRMINGHAM: in Midlands, industry, colloquially known as 'Brum'
BLACKPOOL: popular seaside town, NW England
BRIGHTON: popular seaside resort for Londoners, S. coast
CAMBRIDGE: old university town on R. Cam, 80km. N of London
CANTERBURY: old cathedral city, SE England
CARDIFF: port, industry, capital of Wales
DOVER: Channel port, known for castle & white cliffs
DUBLIN: on R. Liffey, capital of Republic of Ireland
EDINBURGH: castle, arts festival, Scottish capital
GLASGOW: industrial city in Scotland, W. of Edinburgh
JOHN O'GROATS: northernmost point of mainland Britain
LIVERPOOL: port, industry, NW England, W. of Manchester
LONDON: capital of Britain, on R.Thames, pop. 7 mill.
MANCHESTER: large industrial city in N of England
NEWCASTLE: port, industry, NE England, people called 'Geordies'
OXFORD: old university town on R. Thames 90kms NW of London

STRATFORD-ON-AVON: Shakespeare's birthplace, S. of Birmingham
WINDSOR: town, royal castle, on R. Thames, 25kms W. of London

Islands/Lakes/Rivers (36-48)

RIVER AVON: runs through Stratford to join R. Severn
CHANNEL ISLES: Jersey, Guernsey, Alderney, Sark, near France (used to be French), British but not in UK
RIVER CLYDE: 171 kms, runs through Glasgow
HEBRIDES: islands off W. coast of Scotland
LOCH LOMOND: largest lake in Scotland, just N. of Glasgow
ISLE OF MAN: between Britain & Ireland, tourism/motor cycle racing, British but not in UK, adjective: 'Manx'
LOCH NESS: Scottish lake which may contain a monster
ORKNEYS: group of islands just off N. Scotland
SCILLY ISLES: off SW England, tourism & flower growing
RIVER SEVERN: longest in Britain (338 kms), rises in Wales
SHETLANDS: islands 80 kms NE of Orkneys, oil industry centre
RIVER THAMES: runs through Oxford, Windsor, London to the sea
ISLE OF WIGHT: off English S. coast, seaside & sailing

High Areas (49-57)

BEN NEVIS: highest peak in Britain (1343m), in W. Scotland
COTSWOLDS: beautiful range of hills in W. Midlands
DARTMOOR: area of moors & hills in SW England
HIGHLANDS: mountains in W. Scotland
LAKE DISTRICT: beautiful mountains & lakes, NW England
PEAK DISTRICT: central England, good for climbing/walking
PENNINES: mountains running down centre of N. of England
SNOWDONIA: mountain area, N. Wales, highest peak: Snowdon (1085m)
YORKSHIRE MOORS: wild, open, hilly region in NE England

Other Geographical Features (58-61)

FENS: flat, marshy area in E. England
LAND'S END: rocky beauty spot, extreme SW. point of mainland Britain
SALISBURY PLAIN: empty, flat area in SW. England, famous for prehistoric Stonehenge, 130 kms. W. of London
THE WASH: very large bay on central E. coast of England

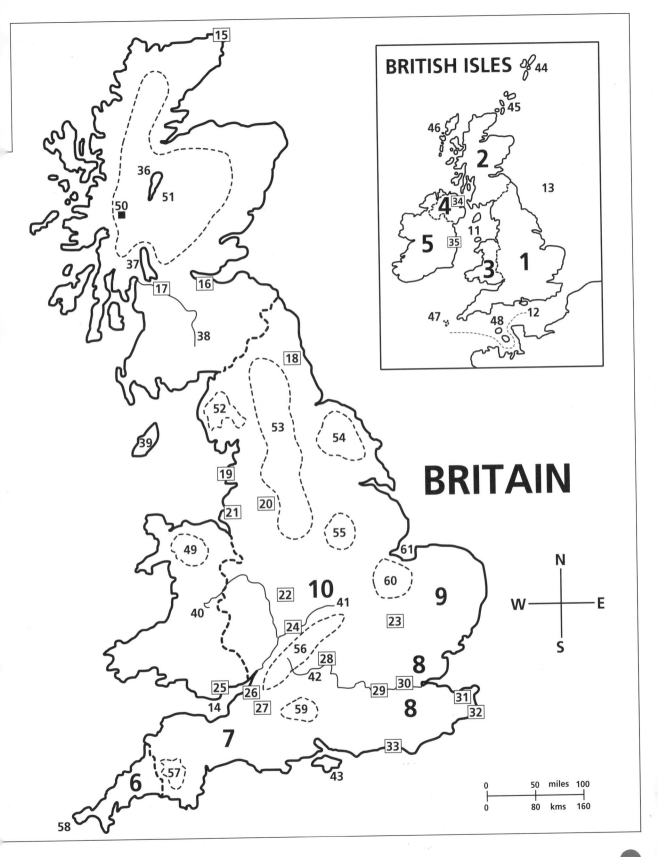

BRITISH ISLES

BRITAIN

N
W — E
S

0   50 miles 100
0   80 kms 160

Word Building

Prefixes

In the following exercises syllables or words are to be added to the front of other words to change or add to their meaning. Where necessary, hyphens have been placed in the sentences.

1   **co-**(with, together) **re-**(again) **ex-**(former, before) **inter-**(between)

Put one of the above prefixes in each of the spaces in the sentences below.

(a)   The _____-pilot took over the plane's controls while the captain had a coffee and sandwich.

(b)   The US and Russia have the capacity to attack each other with _____ -continental missiles.

(c)   Germany and France are _____-operating on the design of a new space-rocket.

(d)   She's divorced but she's still on good terms with her _____-husband.

(e)   Does _____national sport really improve relations between countries?

(f)   The teacher told his student to _____write his bad composition.

(g)   The local trains are slow but the _____-city services are excellent.

(h)   Most houses need to be _____painted every five to seven years.

(i)   Men who once served in the armed services are called _____-servicemen.

(j)   Both boys and girls go to that school. It's _____-educational.

2   **bi-**(two) **pre-**(before) **semi-**(half) **counter-**(in the opposite direction)

Instructions as above.

(a)   We managed to drive the enemy back, but they _____attacked.

(b)   The back wheel of a _____cycle bears more weight than the front wheel.

(c)   Dinosaurs lived millions of years ago in _____historic times.

(d)   The pupils' desks were arranged in a _____circle round the teacher.

(e)   His father is Greek and his mother is Italian so he's _____lingual.

(f)   It was a _____lateral agreement, signed by India and Pakistan.

(g)   Libby is three. She goes to a _____-school playgroup every morning.

(h)   The _____espionage department has caught three foreign spies.

(i)   Houses in Britain are often built in pairs. They're called _____-detached.

(j)   He was only _____-conscious when the ambulance arrived and he died in hospital.

3   **post-**(after) **mono-**(one) **anti-**(against) **non-**(not)

Instructions as above.

(a)   He got his university degree last year. Now he's doing _____graduate studies.

(b)   Some flights go from London to the Middle East _____-stop.

(c)   The words 'fat', 'help' and 'come' are all _____syllables.

(d)   That's _____sense! You don't know what you're talking about!

(e)   The principal _____-war problem was to rebuild the destroyed cities and industries.

(f)   Maybe future trains will run on just a single rail. This system is called a _____rail.

(g) To prevent petrol from freezing, put _____freeze in the tank.
(h) I'm not _____-marriage. I think it's a very good custom.
(i) I'm afraid the club is not open to _____-members.

4 **multi-(many) trans-(across) super-(above, more than) de-(acting against)**

Instructions as above.

(a) The countryside is becoming _____forested so quickly that soon there'll be no trees left at all.
(b) He works in London and in New York so he's a regular _____atlantic air passenger.
(c) The train became _____railed at 60 miles per hour but no one was seriously hurt.
(d) He was so powerful that he sometimes seemed almost _____human.
(e) It is now possible to _____plant a heart from a dead person to a living one.
(f) Britain has people from all over the world. It's a _____racial society.
(g) The villages are becoming _____populated as more and more people move to the cities.
(h) He believes in ghosts and magic and other _____ natural things.
(i) Concorde is a _____sonic plane. It flies faster than sound.
(j) He's incredibly rich. He's certainly a _____-millionaire.

5 **pro-(for, in favour of) sub-(under) uni-(one) tri-(three)**

Instructions as above.

(a) That road is very dangerous. Use the _____way to get across.
(b) That newspaper is very left-wing. In fact it's _____-communist.
(c) The _____marine approached the warship unseen.
(d) They have discovered some _____terranean caves 200 feet down.
(e) Soldiers, policemen and firemen wear _____form. Teachers don't.
(f) Small children ride _____cycles, not bicycles.
(g) He likes British people and culture. He's very _____-British.
(h) A shape with three angles is called a _____angle.
(i) The _____-war party wanted more arms and a bigger army.
(j) Both men and women have their hair cut there. It's a _____sex salon.

6 **over-(too much) under-(not enough)**

Put one of the above prefixes in each of the spaces in the sentences below.

(a) He needs a good holiday. He's suffering from _____work.
(b) She didn't hear the alarm clock and _____slept.
(c) It needs to be cooked a little more. It's _____done.
(d) You've _____charged me. The price is £8 not £10.
(e) They say they're _____paid and want more money.
(f) There aren't enough people in the country. It's _____populated.
(g) There were too many people in the room. It was _____crowded.
(h) Rich nations should give more aid to _____developed countries.
(i) He's fat and lazy. It's because he _____eats.
(j) We _____estimated the cost of the holiday and ran out of money.

7 un- dis-

Put one of the above prefixes n each space in the phrases below to make the word which follows it opposite in meaning.

(a) a(n) _____comfortable chair
(b) a(n) _____believable story
(c) a(n) _____punctual train
(d) a(n) _____respectful pupil
(e) a(n) _____popular man
(f) a(n) _____honest shopkeeper
(g) a(n) _____lucky accident
(h) a(n) _____familiar city
(i) a(n) _____satisfied customer
(j) a(n) _____grateful child
(k) a(n) _____united party

(l) to _____lock a door
(m) to _____obey an order
(n) to _____believe a story
(o) to _____ agree with someone
(p) to _____load a ship
(q) to _____approve of someone
(r) to _____like cheese
(s) to _____appear round the corner
(t) to _____button a jacket
(u) to _____cover buried treasure
(v) to _____trust a politician

8 ir- il- im- in-

Put one of the above prefixes in each space in the phrases below to make the word which follows it opposite in meaning.

(a) an _____resistible temptation
(b) an _____possible plan
(c) an _____legal business deal
(d) an _____accurate calculation
(e) an _____mature young man
(f) an _____moral action
(g) an _____convenient arrangement
(h) an _____logical answer
(i) an _____responsible boy
(j) an _____patient motorist
(k) an _____secure feeling

(l) an _____relevant question
(m) an _____polite letter
(n) an _____literate person
(o) _____frequent buses
(p) _____legible handwriting
(q) an _____curable illness
(r) an _____regular train service
(s) an _____dependent country
(t) _____formal clothes
(u) an _____replaceable work of art
(v) an _____expensive present

CATCH-PHRASES

Catch-phrases are expressions which become popular after being used in politics, advertising or television. Some are fashionable for a short time, others remain permanently in the language.

You only live once.
Back to basics.
Give peace a chance.
Here today, gone tomorrow.
If you can't beat them, join them.
If you can't stand the heat, get out of the kitchen.

Suffixes

1 -ish

(i) *-ish* sometimes means 'with the qualities of' e.g. *boyish*.

Put each of the following words in its correct place in the sentences below.

childish girlish amateurish piggish monkish

(a) He lives in one small room and he hasn't many needs. He leads an almost _____ life.
(b) He is usually a very fine actor, but last night he was terrible, really _____.
(c) He's nearly eighteen but he still has very _____ attitudes and interests.
(d) He behaved very badly at lunch. He really has _____ manners.
(e) She still wears rather young, _____ fashions.

(ii) *-ish* often means 'rather', 'about', 'more or less' e.g. *yellowish* (more or less yellow), *eightish* (about eight), *slowish* (rather slow). This use of *-ish* is colloquial, so is not often used in written English.

Put each of the following words in its correct place in the passage below, in which a man who has witnessed a crime describes to a police officer what he saw.

**smallish   sevenish   twentyish   tallish
fairish   greenish   darkish**

Well, it happened very quickly, officer. I was just leaving my office. It was fairly late, perhaps (a) _____ and I couldn't see very well because it was already getting (b) _____. A man came out of the bank. He had (c) _____ hair. His age, well, he was (d) _____ or maybe twenty-five. I couldn't guess his height, but he was (e) _____. He had a suitcase and he got into a car, not a very big one, (f) _____ in fact. The colour? I think it was (g) _____. Sorry I can't be more exact.

2 -ful -less

-ful means 'having', 'with' e.g. *careful, colourful*

-less means 'without', 'lacking' e.g. *careless, windowless*

Put each of the following words in its correct place in the sentences below.

**thoughtful   harmful   successful   friendless
thoughtless   harmless   beautiful   waterless**

(a) The Sahara Desert is a vast _____ area which runs from east to west across Africa.
(b) Smoking is _____ to your health.
(c) This present is just what I want and need. How _____ of you.
(d) I hope you are _____ in your exams.
(e) Don't be afraid of the dog. He's _____.
(f) It was very _____ of you to play the radio so loud so late at night.
(g) She's very _____. Three artists have painted her.
(h) I was alone and _____ in a strange city.

3   -er -ee

-er usually has an active meaning e.g. *examiner* (a person who *examines*, i.e. sets an examination)

-ee usually has a passive meaning e.g. *examinee* (a person who *is examined*, i.e. takes an examination)

Put each of the following words in its correct place in the sentences below.

interviewer	**trainer**	**employer**
interviewee	**trainee**	**employee**

(a) I was given a pay rise of £1,000 by my _____.
(b) A football team normally has a _____ to keep the players fit.
(c) A television _____ should always give the _____ a proper chance to express his or her opinions.
(d) That company has 200 people working in its factory. My brother works there and I, too, am an _____.
(e) At the moment he's a management _____. If he's successful, he'll be given his first responsible position in January.

4   -proof

-proof means 'safe against', 'able to resist' e.g. *a fireproof door.*

Put each of the following words in its correct place in the sentences below.

waterproof	**soundproof**	**bulletproof**	**heatproof**
shockproof	**childproof**	**foolproof**	

(a) The windows of the President's car were made of _____ glass in case of an assassination attempt.
(b) Our tent wasn't completely _____ and the rain came through.
(c) The soldiers were given _____ watches.
(d) These dishes are _____. You can put them in the oven.
(e) The bank's security system is completely _____. It can't possibly go wrong.
(f) The car locks should be _____, otherwise my young sons will open them during a journey and fall out.
(g) The recording studio was completely _____.

5   -ful

-ful is often used to indicate quantity e.g. *a pocketful* (the contents of a pocket) of coins.

Put each of the following words in its correct place in the sentences below.

houseful	**cupful**	**tankful**
handful	**mouthful**	**teaspoonful**

(a) Put a large _____ of rice in boiling water, then add a little salt, just a _____.
(b) At Christmas we had a _____ of visitors.
(c) The foreign tourist put a _____ of money in front of the taxi driver and said, 'Is this enough?'
(d) After just one _____ I knew she was a wonderful cook.
(e) A _____ of petrol should take this car over 200 miles.

6 -er -or -ar

From the verbs below make nouns describing people by adding -er, -or or -ar to the end and making any other necessary spelling changes.

e.g. liberate *liberator*   drum *drummer*

(a) teach	(h) murder	(o) work
(b) direct	(i) operate	(p) donate
(c) beg	(j) demonstrate	(q) visit
(d) interpret	(k) inspect	(r) produce
(e) translate	(l) act	(s) travel
(f) collect	(m) buy	(t) compete
(g) sail	(n) edit	

7 Instructions as above.

(a) sing	(h) supply	(o) photograph
(b) govern	(i) control	(p) swim
(c) announce	(j) investigate	(q) contribute
(d) admire	(k) ski	(r) create
(e) decorate	(l) instruct	(s) manage
(f) rob	(m) elect	(t) lie
(g) survive	(n) write	

8 -ist -ian

From the nouns below make other nouns describing people by adding -ist or -ian to the end and making any other necessary spelling changes.

e.g. Brazil *Brazilian*   violin *violinist*

(a) motor	(i) art	(q) magic
(b) electricity	(j) bicycle	(r) flower
(c) Paris	(k) guitar	(s) comedy
(d) Christ	(l) politics	(t) beauty
(e) piano	(m) science	(u) journal
(f) history	(n) music	(v) parachute
(g) Buddha	(o) psychiatry	(w) language
(h) economy	(p) terror	(x) archaeology

JARGON

Jargon is the language of a particular profession or occupation. The specialized vocabulary means that it is often incomprehensible to ordinary people. Here are two examples.

'Clamp a redhead with a sheet of half-blue onto the magic arm, close down the barn doors and bounce the light off a sheet of poly.' (film-making)

'Chomsky's transformational-generative grammar essentially looks at syntax but it incorporates more than Phrase-structure grammar does, and includes both phonology and semantics.' (language-teaching)

Nouns made from Verbs

1   -sis -ure

Make nouns ending in -sis or -ure from the following verbs, making any necessary changes in spelling. Then put each noun in its correct place in the sentences below.

emphasize	hypnotize	sign	analyse	paralyse
seize	diagnose	fail	close	enclose

(a) The doctor's _____ was that I had bronchitis.
(b) Don't put an _____ inside an aerogramme. It is not permitted.
(c) The _____ of the blood will help the police find the murderer.
(d) The doctor used _____ to make her calm and relaxed.
(e) He was very ambitious, and his _____ to become prime minister was a shock to him.
(f) The _____ at the bottom of the letter was impossible to read.
(g) Some teachers put a lot of _____ on learning by heart.
(h) There has been a military government since the army's _____ of power six years ago.
(i) This disease can lead to the _____ of certain muscles.
(j) The _____ of the factory and loss of jobs came as a result of fewer orders from abroad.

2   -y

Make nouns from the following verbs by adding -y to the end and making any other necessary changes in spelling. Then put each noun in its correct place in the sentences below.

prosper	enquire	injure	discover	apologize	forge
expire	deliver	recover	conspire	assemble	

(a) In England there is no postal _____ on Sundays.
(b) He still suffers from an _____ he received in a game of football ten years ago.
(c) He cold copy other people's signatures perfectly. He was finally sent to prison for _____.
(d) The _____ of a ship from the bottom of the sea is a very difficult, expensive operation.
(e) The _____ of America was made in 1492 by Christopher Colombus.
(f) I wish you happiness, good health and _____ for this coming year.
(g) This is the parliamentary building, where the National _____ meets.
(h) She accepted his _____ for his rude behaviour at dinner.
(i) The President believed there was a _____ to overthrow him.
(j) On _____, your passport may be renewed for a further five years.
(k) Thank you for your _____ about our products. We enclose our current catalogue.

3   -ence

Make nouns ending in -ence from the following verbs, making any necessary changes in spelling. Then put each noun in its correct place in the sentences below.

prefer   **obey**   **defend**   **offend**   **insist**   **coincide**
refer   **depend**   **correspond**   **reside**   **differ**   **interfere**
exist   **pretend**

(a)   He couldn't go to university but continued his education through _____ courses.
(b)   This monument is in memory of the men and women who died in _____ of this country.
(c)   Police dogs are trained to a high standard of _____.
(d)   Tea or coffee? Do you have any _____?
(e)   She wasn't really angry at all. It was just _____.
(f)   Dictionaries, encyclopaedias and atlases are called _____ books.
(g)   The doctors tried to cure him of his _____ on drugs.
(h)   The United Nations came into _____ in 1945.
(i)   Despite his _____ that he was innocent, he was arrested.
(j)   I can't tell the _____ between butter and margarine.
(k)   I hope she didn't take _____. I was only joking.
(l)   I met John on holiday quite by chance. What a _____.
(m) She complained of _____ by her mother-in-law in her private affairs.
(n)   'Place of _____' means the place where you live.

4   -ance

Make nouns from the following verbs by adding -ance to the end and making any other necessary changes in spelling. Then put each noun in its correct place in the sentences below.

annoy   **resist**   **avoid**   **insure**   **resemble**   **enter**
attend   **perform**   **accept**   **disturb**   **assist**   **endure**

(a)   It was the actor's finest _____.
(b)   The teacher kept a record of every student's _____.
(c)   This signature bears no _____ to mine! It's a forgery!
(d)   When I received the offer of a job, I immediately wrote a letter of _____.
(e)   The police were called to a _____ at a private party last night.
(f)   My house _____ covers me for fire, flood, theft and damage.
(g)   When she was very old she couldn't look after herself without _____.
(h)   When people kept talking during the film, he showed his _____ by turning round and looking at them.
(i)   The _____ to the park is through that gate there.
(j)   After fierce _____ for two days, the soldiers surrendered to the enemy.
(k)   By continuing his journey alone, on foot, in freezing weather without food for two days he showed remarkable powers of _____.
(l)   The Automobile Association recommends _____ of the city centre during the present road repairs.

5 -al

Make nouns from the following verbs by adding -al to the end and making any other necessary changes in spelling. Then put each noun in its correct place in the sentences below.

deny	propose	approve	bury	refuse	try
renew	remove	arrive	survive	dismiss	rehearse

(a) His unpunctuality and bad work soon led to his _____ from the firm.
(b) After the funeral service in the church, we went out to the cemetery for the _____.
(c) Thousands of people were at the airport for the President's _____.
(d) _____ of your season ticket for another six months will cost you £268.
(e) To get married before you are eighteen, you will need your parents' _____ and consent.
(f) The first performance of the play is tomorrow. The actors are having a final _____ tonight.
(g) At the end of the five-day _____, he was found guilty and sent to prison.
(h) The factory manager wants to use different machines but the workers don't like this _____.
(i) The police were amazed at the _____ of the five children after a night out in freezing temperatures.
(j) He made a complete _____ of the accusation against him but no one believed him.
(k) I don't understand his _____ to help us. He's usually very helpful.
(l) The new republican government demanded the _____ of the king's statue from the main square.

6 -age

Make nouns from the following verbs by adding -age to the end and making any other necessary changes in spelling. Then put each noun in its correct place in the sentences below.

use	shrink	store	post	stop
break	wreck	marry	leak	pass

(a) A family house always needs _____ space for old furniture and luggage.
(b) With the _____ of time, her heartache grew less painful.
(c) The _____ between Alan and Josephine will take place in St Andrew's Church on April 21st.
(d) The firm is proud of its non-strike record. There hasn't been a _____ of work for twelve years.
(e) Airmail _____ to Australia for a large parcel is very expensive.
(f) The _____ of the smashed car was left by the road as a warning to motorists.
(g) The Prime Minister is very angry about the _____ of information to the press from closed secret meetings.
(h) The American _____ of this word is different from the British.
(i) In a shop selling glass and china a certain amount of _____ is unavoidable.
(j) This shirt was guaranteed against _____, but look, it's too small for me now and I've only washed it once.

7 Put in each space below a noun formed from the verb in brackets after the sentence.

(a) John's an expert, so I asked him for some _____. (advise)

(b) You need more _____ before you can play the violin in public. (practise)

(c) The policeman wanted to see the motorist's driving _____. (license).

(d) He made a _____ that she would marry and have three children. (prophesy)

(e) We can only get there by plane. There's no _____. (choose)

(f) 'Now children, I hope you'll all be on your best _____ when we go to the museum.' (behave)

(g) I have to make a _____ about poor service and the rudeness of your staff. (complain)

(h) I think you've made an _____ in the bill. Could you check it? (err)

(i) Naturally he's very unhappy at the _____ of so much money. (lose)

(j) I like a museum with a _____ of objects – pictures, sculpture, furniture and other things. (mix)

(k) The company has shown rapid _____ in the last two years. (grow)

8 Instructions as above.

(a) Newspapers in that country can say what they like. There's no _____. (censor)

(b) It took him a long time to recover from the _____ of his mother. (die)

(c) The _____ of poverty, disease and ignorance must be our principal aim. (conquer)

(d) It is my _____ that there is life on mars and Venus. (believe)

(e) The police think that she committed the murder but they have no _____. (prove)

(f) It was a great _____ to hear that your illness isn't serious. (relieve)

(g) Most of the passengers were killed in the aircrash. The _____ were badly injured. (remain)

(h) Two miles from here, it's still possible to see the _____ of a 2,000-year-old Roman town. (remain)

(i) Some people tie a knot in their handkerchiefs as a _____ of something important they must do. (remind)

(j) The priest asked us to say a _____ for world peace. (pray)

(k) He put the two televisions together so that we could make a _____. (compare)

9 Instructions as above.

(a) The police car crashed into a traffic-light while it was in _____ of a stolen car. (pursue)

(b) He feels a deep _____ for the people who killed his brother. (hate)

(c) Of course the _____ of a mountain takes longer than the _____. (ascend ... descend)

(d) Not far from here you can see the _____ of an old church. Only the walls are left. (ruin)

(e) If you want to know what's in a book, look at the _____ page at the front. (contain)

(f) He has a very wide _____ of African affairs. (know)

(g) You'll have to make a _____ soon. (decide)

(h) She's very nice but she has a _____ to talk too much. (tend)

(i) I'm not sure, but I have a _____ that he was the boy who stole my bike. (suspect)

(j)   The actors received enthusiastic _____ at the end of the show. (applaud)
(k)   The staff at this hotel are excellent. They give very good _____. (serve)
(l)   The _____ of the new baby was about four kilograms. (weigh)
(m)   We believe the existence of large armies and terrible weapons is a _____ to world peace. (threaten)
(n)   His first _____ missed but he killed the bird with his second. (shoot)
(o)   £50,000 was taken in the bank _____ yesterday. (rob)
(p)   I've written three letters to the firm about their bad product, but they've made no _____. (respond)

10   -sion

Make nouns, all ending in *-sion,* from the following verbs. Put each noun in its correct place in the sentences below.

divide	**conclude**	**expand**
persuade	**revise**	**admit** .
exclude	**explode**	**include**

(a)   I hope friendly _____ will make him change his mind. I don't want to use force.
(b)   If they get divorced, they'll have to decide on the _____ of their money and property.
(c)   He dreamt of the _____ of his firm from a small factory to a large international business.
(d)   _____ to the club is limited to members only.
(e)   There was a very loud _____ when the bomb went off.
(f)   In the final weeks before the exam, the students did a lot of _____.
(g)   He was delighted by his _____ in the national football team.
(h)   The _____ of her name from the list of people chosen to meet the President was a great disappointment.
(i)   ... and finally, in _____, I thank you all for coming.

11   Instructions as above.

possess	**confuse**	**permit**
discuss	**invade**	**collide**
confess	**extend**	**impress**

(a)   The _____ of the island was resisted as soon as the soldiers landed on the beaches.
(b)   His car was slightly damaged in the _____.
(c)   Pupils must not enter the teachers' room without _____.
(d)   His dirty appearance made a bad _____ on the judge.
(e)   He was arrested for _____ of illegal drugs.
(f)   The police questioned him for three days until he finally made a _____.
(g)   Three boys in the school had the same name, which caused some _____.
(h)   During the office meeting there was a _____ about the need for a new photocopier.
(i)   He asked for an _____ of his visa for another six months.

12 -ment

Make nouns from the following verbs by adding *-ment* to the end. Put each noun in its correct place in the sentences below.

entertain	**improve**	**postpone**	**arrange**
enlarge	**encourage**	**advertise**	

(a) The _____ for Monday is that we'll meet at 7 and take the train at 7.45.
(b) I like this photo. I think I'll have an _____ made.
(c) This is the city's _____ district, full of cinemas and theatres.
(d) We regret to announce the _____ of this evening's concert. The conductor is ill. The concert will take place next week.
(e) The teachers were pleased at the _____ in his work.
(f) His parents gave him a lot of _____ in his studies.
(g) There was a newspaper _____ for a job as a typist.

13 Instructions as above.

imprison	**manage**	**disappoint**	**develop**	**punish**
announce	**treat**	**govern**	**employ**	**agree**

(a) The _____ has announced new, higher taxes.
(b) 'Capital _____' means the death penalty.
(c) The company _____ had talks with the workers' representatives but they couldn't reach _____.
(d) A lot of country people without jobs came to the city to look for _____.
(e) He received _____ at the hospital for his injuries.
(f) It was a big _____ to hear that you can't come to our wedding.
(g) She was sentenced to three years' _____.
(h) Television programmes were interrupted by a special _____ about the plane crash.
(i) I hope that we will soon see the _____ of better relations between our two countries.

14 -tion

Make nouns ending in *-tion* from the following verbs, making any necessary spelling changes. Then put each noun in its correct place in the sentences below.

revolt	**repeat**	**compete**	**reduce**	**acquire**
pronounce	**produce**	**qualify**	**solve**	**introduce**

(a) There's a lot of _____ among car manufacturers to sell most cars.
(b) There are some differences in _____ between British and American English.
(c) Is a degree a necessary _____ for this job?
(d) _____ of the new sports car has been affected by a fire at the factory.
(e) They are trying to find a _____ to the problem.
(f) A book sometimes sells better if it has an _____ written by a famous person.
(g) The art gallery is very proud of its recent _____ of an important painting.
(h) There was a _____. The people rose up and overthrew the government.
(i) That must not happen again. There must be no _____ of the incident.
(j) That shop is offering a big _____ in the price of its clothes.

15 Instructions as above.

satisfy	oppose	explain	publish	abolish
receive	describe	destroy	deceive	detain

(a) The earthquake caused the complete _____ of the village.
(b) The party, or parties, against the government is called the _____.
(c) He's finished writing his new book. _____ will be next year.
(d) The new film has had a very poor _____ by the critics.
(e) She did not get the money honestly and legally. She got it by _____.
(f) Many people would like to see the _____ of all nuclear weapons.
(g) He had to give his boss an _____ for his absence.
(h) Seven illegal immigrants are being held in _____ at the port.
(i) His work is well-paid but doesn't give him much _____.
(j) If you send us a _____ of the missing property, we'll try to find it.

16 -ion

Make nouns from the following verbs by adding -ion to the end. Put each noun in its correct place in the sentences below.

prevent	interrupt	elect	protect	suggest
predict	select	react	invent	addict

(a) If I can work all day without any _____, I can finish the job by this evening.
(b) I can't make any _____ about the _____ result. I don't know how the voting will go.
(c) What was his _____ to the news? Was he pleased or angry?
(d) RSPCA stands for the Royal Society for the _____ of Cruelty to Animals.
(e) His _____ of a new type of car engine brought him a lot of money.
(f) His _____ to drugs nearly killed him.
(g) RSPB stands for the Royal Society for the _____ of Birds.
(h) What shall we do tomorrow? Swimming? Film? Museum? Has anyone got a better _____?
(i) He was delighted by his _____ for the school football team.

17 -ation

In each space below put a noun ending in -ation made from the verb in brackets below the phrase.

(a) a police _____ (investigate)
(b) a wild _____ (exaggerate)
(c) a heart _____ (operate)
(d) _____ leather (imitate)
(e) good _____ (pronounce)
(f) the manager's _____ (resign)
(g) a _____ stone (found)
(h) _____ links (communicate)
(i) a vivid _____ (imagine)
(j) a serious _____ (accuse)
(k) the _____ of a meeting (cancel)
(l) I'm full of _____ (admire)
(m) the _____ of words (abbreviate)
(n) exam _____ (prepare)
(o) a political _____ (demonstrate)
(p) state or private _____ (educate)
(q) _____ from poor countries (emigrate)
(r) _____ to rich countries (immigrate)

18 Instructions as above.

(a) a _____ to charity (donate)
(b) a moment's _____ (hesitate)
(c) a car with good _____ (accelerate)
(d) a hotel _____ (reserve)
(e) a burning _____ (sense)
(f) a _____ of song and dance (combine)
(g) a police _____ (interrogate)
(h) a party _____ (invite)
(i) _____ of her health (deteriorate)
(j) a school _____ (examine)
(k) a timetable _____ (alter)
(l) tourist _____ (inform)
(m) an evening's _____ (relax)
(n) _____ of old paintings (restore)
(o) I resisted the _____ (tempt)
(p) the _____ of a story (continue)
(q) a journey of _____ (explore)
(r) the _____ of a book (translate)
(s) the _____ of a speech (interpret)
(t) careful _____ (punctuate)

LIFE TRENDS

New technology and social trends have brought innovations into modern life
and new expressions into the language. Do you know all the following?

women's liberation
organ transplants
teleshopping
hair implants
phone help-lines
cycleways

animal rights groups
recycling (paper, glass, tin)
drug rehabilitation units
surveillance cameras
audio books (for the blind)
ecological groups

Nouns made from Adjectives

1 Put in each space below a noun made from the adjective in brackets after the sentence.

(a) South Africa has great mineral _____. (wealthy)

(b) _____ is one of the world's great problems. (poor)

(c) Tell the _____. (true)

(d) I must drink something. I'm dying of _____. (thirsty)

(e) I must eat something. I'm dying of _____. (hungry)

(f) He was very bright. He passed the exam with _____. (easy)

(g) In his _____ he travelled a lot. Now he is too old. (young)

(h) I don't know how to express my _____ for your help. (grateful)

(i) It's very late. There's not much _____ of his coming now. (likely)

(j) To be a soldier you need to be strong and in good _____. (healthy)

(k) There was no doubt about his _____. He was sent to prison for five years. (guilty)

(l) He escaped to _____ by climbing over the prison wall. (free)

2 Instructions as above.

(a) The _____ of the president was announced on the radio. (dead)

(b) In past wars soldiers were sometimes shot for _____. (cowardly)

(c) He died to save the lives of others. It was an act of _____. (heroic)

(d) He was a very thoughtful, philosophical person. A man of great _____. (wise)

(e) She felt great _____ at being treated so badly. (angry)

(f) He left his town to find _____ in the big city. (famous)

(g) The tourists were impressed by the _____ of the jewellery in the museum. (splendid)

(h) It was a long, slow film. I nearly died of _____. (boring)

(i) He was filled with _____ at the terrible things he saw in the war. (horrible)

(j) The ice quickly melted in the _____ of the sun. (hot)

(k) His _____ was hurt when a younger man was given the job above him. (proud)

(l) I think it shows _____ of character to admit you are wrong. (strong)

3 Instructions as above.

(a) To be successful you need ability and you need _____. (lucky)

(b) He was delighted by the _____ of the welcome he received. (warm)

(c) The idea of going through the forest alone at night filled her with _____. (terrible)

(d) The _____ of the bridge is about two kilometres. (long)

(e) The _____ of the road is not great enough to take large trucks. (wide)

(f) What's the _____ of that mountain? (high)

(g) The _____ of the water here is over three metres. (deep)

4 -ence -ance

Make nouns ending in -ence or -ance from the following adjectives and put them in their correct places in the sentences below.

confident	independent	patient	innocent	absent
intelligent	important	silent	elegant	present
convenient	reluctant	violent	arrogant	

(a) The police were there to prevent any possible _____.
(b) There was complete _____ except for the sound of the birds.
(c) He was very unsure of himself. He didn't have much _____.
(d) She dressed with great _____ in clothes of the latest French fashions.
(e) Although he maintained his _____ to the end, he was sent to prison.
(f) It doesn't matter. It's of no _____.
(g) What a silly thing to do. I thought he had more _____.
(h) He thinks he's the only person who's right! What _____!
(i) Zimbabwe gained its _____ in 1975.
(j) He didn't like school, and went every day with great _____.
(k) Please have a little _____. We must wait another hour.
(l) Please send the goods at your earliest _____.
(m) The boss didn't believe that her _____ was due to illness.
(n) People normally stand in the _____ of the Queen.

5 -cy

Make nouns ending in -cy from the following adjectives and put them in their correct places in the sentences below.

obstinate	private	urgent	efficient
accurate	vacant	frequent	fluent

(a) Swiss watches are famous for their _____.
(b) A _____ for an office manager was advertised in the newspaper.
(c) This is a matter of great _____. It must be discussed as soon as possible.
(d) Donkeys are known for their _____. They won't do what they're told.
(e) After five years in London, of course he speaks English with great _____.
(f) He always did his job well. Everyone appreciated his _____.
(g) The _____ of this bus service is about one every ten minutes.
(h) I don't like to be visited or phoned too much at home. I like my _____.

6 -ity -ness

Make nouns from the following adjectives by adding -ity or -ness to the end, and put them in their correct places in the sentences below.

punctual	bald	deaf	foolish
similar	equal	quiet	popular

(a) He's worried about his increasing _____. He might get a wig.
(b) What _____ to leave a baby out in the hot sun.
(c) The teacher insisted on _____.
(d) Men and women should have _____ of pay and opportunity.
(e) I have some _____ in my left ear.
(f) The international _____ of the Beatles was amazing.
(g) I like the _____ of this street. It's very peaceful.
(h) There is some _____ between German and Dutch.

7 Instructions as above.

stupid	formal	weak	neutral	neat	real
fond	serious	superior	Christian	ill	blunt

(a) Don't laugh! I don't think you understand the _____ of the situation.
(b) The principal religion of this area is _____.
(c) The teacher gave a special mark for _____.
(d) He proved his _____ by winning easily.
(e) Switzerland has a record of _____ in past wars.
(f) He spoke with such _____ that many people were offended.
(g) _____ kept him away from work for a week.
(h) I was surprised by the _____ of the occasion. All the men wore dark suits and ties.
(i) Engineers have found a _____ in the bridge. They'll have to strengthen it.
(j) The French _____ for wine is well known. They like it a lot.
(k) He is always daydreaming; he never faces _____.
(l) What a crazy thing to do. How could anyone behave with such _____?

8   -ty

Make nouns ending in -ty from the following adjectives, making any necessary spelling changes, then put them in their correct places in the sentences below.

curious	vain	simple	anxious	brief
generous	necessary	clear	gay	various

(a) He spoke with great _____. Everyone understood.
(b) There's no _____ to take the exam if you don't want to.
(c) We were disappointed by the _____ of our stay in Paris. Two days was not enough.
(d) The children looked at the foreign stranger with _____.
(e) There is increasing _____ about the missing children.
(f) He is famous for his _____. He gives large sums to charity.
(g) In spite of his fame, wealth and success, he lives a life of great _____.
(h) He's always looking at himself in the mirror. What _____!
(i) In a big city like Amsterdam there's always a _____ of things to do in the evening.
(j) The music, dancing and decoration gave the party an atmosphere of great _____.

EUPHEMISMS

A euphemism is a word or phrase we use to avoid referring too directly to something unpleasant or embarrassing. Can you guess the meaning of these?

My grandfather **passed on** two years ago.
He's **being economical with the truth.**
The doctor says your mother **is in a bad way.**
Excuse me. I have to **spend a penny.**
Joe **had one too many** in the pub last night.

9   -y

Make nouns ending in *-y* from the following adjectives, making any necessary spelling changes, then put them in their correct places in the sentences.

tragic	**courteous**	**jealous**	**envious**	**hypocritical**
certain	**beautiful**	**difficult**	**furious**	**safe**
loyal	**royal**	**cruel**		

(a)   '_____' is another word for 'politeness'.
(b)   NSPCC stands for the National Society for the Prevention of _____ to Children.
(c)   The Scottish Highlands are full of great natural _____.
(d)   '_____' and '_____' mean more or less the same.
(e)   During the bombing, children were taken to a place of _____.
(f)   The newspapers described the deaths in the air crash as a _____.
(g)   At first he had great _____ in understanding the language.
(h)   That entrance is reserved for _____ and other important people.
(i)   People reacted with _____ to the President's speech and thousands of people attacked his palace.
(j)   He says everyone is equal but he treats his employees badly. What _____!
(k)   I think they'll arrive tomorrow but no one is sure. There's not much _____ about it.
(l)   His wife supported him through all his troubles. She showed great _____.

10   -iness

Make nouns ending in *-iness* from the following adjectives, making any necessary spelling changes, then put them in their correct places below.

happy	**tidy**	**ugly**	**holy**
lazy	**lonely**	**naughty**	**lovely**

(a)   Living alone in the city, he suffered from _____ at first.
(b)   A factory can be attractive. It doesn't have to be a place of _____.
(c)   The birth of their baby daughter brought them a lot of _____.
(d)   He lost his job because of his _____.
(e)   Please respect the _____ of this religious place by not talking loudly.
(f)   Their mother punished them for their _____ in breaking the window and telling lies.
(g)   The teacher complimented her pupils on their _____. They had all polished their shoes and combed their hair.
(h)   The _____ of the view almost took my breath away.

11   -ion -ment

Make nouns ending in *-ion* or *-ment* from the following adjectives, making any necessary spelling changes, then put them in their correct places below.

cautious	**attractive**	**perfect**	**tense**	**content**	**excited**

(a)   After the revolution people were nervous about going into the streets. There was an atmosphere of _____.
(b)   She dances so beautifully she almost reaches _____.
(c)   In his old age he lives a life of peace, comfort and _____.
(d)   This animal is dangerous. It should be handled with the greatest _____.
(e)   The children's _____ increased as Christmas Day drew near.
(f)   The Eiffel Tower in Paris is a major tourist _____.

Adjectives made from Nouns

1 -y -ly

The addition of -y or -ly to a noun often makes an adjective,

e.g. a *windy night, fatherly advice,* a *daily newspaper.*

Put each of the following words in its correct place in the sentences below.

salty	**grassy**	**scholarly**	**rainy**
friendly	**ghostly**	**weekly**	**yearly**

(a) It's a very academic, _____ book.
(b) It's been dry for two weeks but I think next weekend will be _____.
(c) We found a nice _____ place by the river for our picnic.
(d) Julia will help you. She's a very pleasant, _____ girl.
(e) The water of the lake was rather _____, like sea-water.
(f) A _____ figure in white suddenly appeared before us.
(g) He makes _____ visits to his firm's head office in Paris, usually in April.
(h) 'Time' is an American _____ news magazine.

2 -ous

In each space below put an adjective ending in -ous made from the noun in brackets after the phrase.

(a) a _____ plant (poison)
(b) a _____ organisation (religion)
(c) an _____ journey (adventure)
(d) a _____ movement (nerves)
(e) a _____ country (mountain)
(f) a _____ story (humour)
(g) a _____ escape (miracle)
(h) a _____ machine (danger)
(i) a _____ sunset (glory)
(j) an _____ politician (ambition)
(k) a _____ soldier (courage)
(l) a _____ earthquake (disaster)
(m) a _____ film star (fame)
(n) an _____ student (industry)
(o) an _____ disease (infection)
(p) a _____ disappearance (mystery)
(q) a _____ army (victory)
(r) a _____ person (suspicion)

3 -ic

Make adjectives ending in -ic from the following nouns, making any necessary spelling changes, then put them in their correct places below.

democracy	**art**	**drama**	**sympathy**	**climate**
photography	**poetry**	**energy**	**science**	**alcohol**

(a) Whisky of course is an _____ drink.
(b) She paints and draws. She's very _____.
(c) Sweden and Brazil have different weather. They're in different _____ zones.
(d) They have free elections. It's a _____ country.

(e) I feel very fit and _____ today.
(f) She bought a camera and other _____ equipment.
(g) She likes physics, chemistry and other _____ subjects.
(h) He was very patient and _____ when I told him my problem.
(i) She has a very imaginative, _____ style of writing.
(j) The big doors suddenly opened and he entered. It was very _____.

4　-ical

Make adjectives ending in -ical from the following nouns, making any
necessary spelling changes, then put them in their correct places in the
sentences below.

psychology	grammar	crisis	music	politics
medicine	alphabet	clerk	theatre	practice

(a) He speaks Spanish fluently but with some _____ mistakes.
(b) The index at the back of a book is in _____ order.
(c) I never go to concerts. I'm not at all _____.
(d) He's very _____. He can make and repair almost anything.
(e) She could make a lot of money in films, but she is more interested in a _____ career.
(f) He's interested in _____ affairs. He might enter Parliament.
(g) Physically he was unhurt, but he suffered _____ damage.
(h) He treated her injury although he had no _____ qualifications.
(i) The doctors say her condition is now _____.
(j) She wants a _____ job. She has always liked office work.

5　In each space below put an adjective made from the noun in brackets after the phrase.

(a) a _____ dress (fashion)
(b) a _____ army (triumph)
(c) an _____ letter (affection)
(d) a _____ table (circle)
(e) _____ interests (literature)
(f) a _____ house (suburb)
(g) a _____ shape (triangle)
(h) a _____ child (trouble)
(i) a _____ chair (comfort)
(j) a _____ business (profit)
(k) a _____ athlete (muscle)
(l) a _____ painting (value)
(m) a _____ worker (skill)
(n) a _____ state (socialism)
(o) a _____ attempt (success)
(p) a _____ friend (trust)
(q) a _____ place (peace)
(r) a _____ day (memory)
(s) a _____ person (knowledge)
(t) a _____ country (distance)

Adjectives made from Verbs

1 -able

Make adjectives ending in -able from the following verbs, making any necessary spelling changes, then put them in their correct places in the sentences below.

change	advise	accept	suit	adjust	read
enjoy	cure	regret	agree	break	depend

(a) It's _____ to book early, but not essential.
(b) English weather is very _____. It's often different from day to day.
(c) It was a _____ mistake. I am very sorry.
(d) Is 6.30 a _____ time, or is it too early?
(e) He's a very _____ boy. You can rely on him.
(f) Pack them carefully. They're _____.
(g) You'll like it. It's a very _____ book.
(h) You can raise the microphone or lower it. It's _____.
(i) Thank you for a very _____ evening. We had a lovely time.
(j) We regret that late applications are not _____.
(k) We'll meet at 8 if you are all _____.
(l) Fortunately the cancer was _____ and he is now well again.

2 -ive

Make adjectives ending in -ive from the following verbs, making any necessary spelling changes, then put them in their correct places in the sentences below.

destroy	attract	produce	inform	deceive
decide	appreciate	protect	create	talk

(a) He was very _____ of all I had done for him.
(b) The factory has been more _____ since we bought new automatic machines.
(c) His appearance is _____. He's older than he looks.
(d) Nuclear weapons are terribly _____.
(e) His lecture was very _____. We learnt a lot.
(f) She's very _____. She paints, makes sculpture and designs textiles.
(g) She's a very _____ girl. Men always like her.
(h) She was very _____. She told me all about herself and her family.
(i) Firemen wear _____ clothing, otherwise they would get burnt.
(j) He's not afraid to take action. He's very _____.

3

In each space below put an adjective made from the verb in brackets below the phrase.

(a) a _____ body (die)
(b) a _____ book (bore)
(c) an _____ car (economise)
(d) a _____ neighbour (quarrel)
(e) an _____ chapter (introduce)
(f) an _____ film (entertain)
(g) an _____ police officer (observe)
(h) an _____ dog (obey)
(i) a _____ district (reside)
(j) a _____ fish (slip)
(k) an _____ film (educate)
(l) a _____ child (spoil)
(m) a _____ cake (stick)
(n) an _____ leaflet (explain)

Verbs made from Nouns

In each space below put a verb made from the noun in brackets after the sentence.

(a) The teachers _____ the pupils to study. (courage)
(b) I want to _____ my house by building an extra room. (extent)
(c) Fireworks _____ dogs and cats. (fright)
(d) The doctor gave her some tablets to _____ the pain. (relief)
(e) If the ambulance doesn't come soon, he'll _____ to death. (blood)
(f) The police can't _____ that he committed the crime. (proof)
(g) More floods could _____ hundreds of homes. (danger)
(h) The police are trying to _____ the body. (identity)
(i) They plan to _____ the bridge by building more stone supports. (strength)
(j) She said women must _____ themselves from male domination. (liberty)
(k) The smoke was so dense that we could hardly _____. (breath)
(l) My brother and I decided to _____ the money we found. (half)
(m) Why can't they _____ the break so that we have time for a coffee? (length)

Verbs made from Adjectives

-en

Make verbs ending in -en from the following adjectives, making any necessary spelling changes, then put them in their correct places in the sentences below.

tight	less	sweet	loose	deep	straight	weak
flat	worse	sharp	bright	light	ripe	quiet
broad	dark	deaf	wide			

(a) Tomorrow will begin dark and cloudy but it will _____ later.
(b) You can _____ the risk of theft by locking your bicycle.
(c) These apples _____ in June.
(d) You should _____ this dish by adding sugar.
(e) The hospital phoned to warn that her husband's condition was beginning to _____ .
(f) This road is very narrow but they're planning to _____ it.
(g) He managed to _____ the ropes round his wrists and escape.
(h) They decided to _____ the ship by throwing some machinery into the sea.
(i) I don't know how that loud disco music doesn't _____ people.
(j) They are going to _____ that rough area to make a football pitch.
(k) When the evening began to _____, we turned on the lights.
(l) They are going to _____ the harbour so that it can take bigger ships.
(m) Have you a knife? I want to _____ my pencil.
(n) Foreign travel will _____ your experience.
(o) She gave the noisy baby a toy to _____ it.
(p) Can you _____ that picture on the wall. It's crooked.
(q) That screw's loose. _____ it with a screwdriver.
(r) The boxer began the fight strongly but began to _____ in the fifth round.

Specialised Vocabulary

Formal Words

The three passages below are written in formal English. They contain words and structures which are often found in notices, regulations and formal letters but which are not common in ordinary everyday conversation.

1   Put each of the following formal words in its correct place in the notice below.

enquire	produce	facilitate	stating	seek
obligatory	attend	admitted	leave	

ALL COLLEGE STUDENTS

If you wish to obtain a certificate of registration you will be required to (a) _____ your admission slip. A note from your teacher (b) _____ that you (c) _____ your class regularly is not (d) _____ but will greatly (e) _____ matters. If you (f) _____ advice, please (g) _____ at the office. Overseas students should be aware that students are (h) _____ to the college only on condition that they have obtained (i) _____ to study from the Home Office.

---

2   Put each of the following words or phrases in its correct place in the passage below.

provide	terminating	notify	in possession of	additional	further
desire	in excess of	held	retain	locations	prior

Conditions of Car Rental

Drivers must have (a) _____ a valid driving licence for a minimum of three years. Overseas visitors should be (b) _____ a British or International licence.

Cars rented from our London office may only be returned to our other offices (Manchester, Bristol, Oxford) by (c) _____ arrangement and on payment of an (d) _____ charge.

If a driver fails to return a car to us by one week after the agreed (e) _____ date, we will be obliged to inform the police.

Special rates are available for periods (f) _____ three months.

Drivers who (g) _____ to (h) _____ the car for a longer duration should (i) _____ the company as soon as possible.

We also have offices at a number of (j) _____ in Scotland. Our London office will be pleased to (k) _____ (l) _____ details.

---

3   Instructions as above.

funds	commencement	ensure	in duration	commences	departs
prior to	undertake	assist	attire	appropriate	requested

TOUR OF SOUTHERN SPAIN

The tour is fourteen days (a) _____ and (b) _____ on Saturday 11 June, when our luxury coach (c) _____ from our London office. The price, which should be paid at least ten days (d) _____ the (e) _____ of the tour, is inclusive of all transport, meals and accommodation, but travellers should (f) _____ that they take with them adequate (g) _____ for extra expenses.

In the event of the cancellation of the tour we (h) _____ to refund the complete amount paid. The tour group will be accompanied by a courier, who will (i) _____ members of the group at all times.

Travellers are (j) _____ to wear (k) _____ (l) _____ for visits to churches and other holy places.

---

4   Make the following phrases more formal by replacing each word or phrase in italics with a word or phrase from one of the groups in the above three exercises. In some cases it is necessary to make a small change in, or addition to, the words or phrases.

e.g. the train *leaves* at 07.15   the train *departs* at 07.15
we *agree* to do the work   we *undertake* to do the work

(a) *ask* at the station
(b) to *make* things *easier*
(c) *before* our arrival
(d) a *previous* engagement
(e) she will *help* us
(f) *more than* £100
(g) *more* information
(h) *tell* the company
(i) the *beginning* of the course
(j) sufficient *money* for expenses
(k) *keep* your ticket

(l) they'll *give* more information
(m) you must *have* a valid passport
(n) the tour will *end* in Paris
(o) they *go to* a primary school
(p) he was *allowed to enter*
(q) the regulations *say* that ...
(r) if you *want* information
(s) he has *permission* to be absent
(t) *show* your driving licence
(u) *make sure* you have permission
(v) you are *asked* to be punctual

Slang and Colloquial Words

Slang

1 Slang is vocabulary which is used in very informal spoken language but not considered good in formal 'correct' English. For example a slang word for 'thank you' is 'ta' and a slang word for 'mad' is 'nuts'.

The slang words in the sentences below are printed in italics. Replace each slang word with a word or phrase from the following list.

made	friend	television	policeman	discarded	nuisance
pound(s)	cigarettes	alcohol	prison	without money	

(a) He smokes 30 *fags* a day. Too many!
(b) He drinks a lot. He must spend twenty *quid* a week on *booze*.
(c) He thought his meal was overcooked. When the waiter brought his bill he *kicked up* a fuss and would not pay.
(d) I lost £500 at a casino last night. I'm absolutely *skint*.
(e) My *mate* stole a car. Now he's in *the nick*.
(f) She got bored with her boyfriend and *ditched* him.
(g) There's a good film on the *telly* tonight, but I've got to go out. What a *drag!*
(h) I wouldn't like to be a *copper* directing traffic in the street in this bad weather.

Colloquial words

2 Colloquial words are words which are quite acceptable in spoken English but not in written English (except in informal letters to friends etc.). For example we might say, 'He's a nice chap,' but we would probably write, 'He is a pleasant man.' (The line between slang and colloquial words is not at all clear and many words considered colloquial by some people would be considered slang by others.)

The colloquial words in the sentences below are printed in italics. Replace each colloquial word with a word or phrase from the following list.

drunk	very good	child	toilet	short sleep
bicycle	joking	dismiss	without money	upper class
possessions	newspaper			

(a) Her boss said he would *sack* her if she was late again.
(b) There's a *brilliant* film on at the pictures this week.
(c) He made a lot of money and now he lives in a very *posh* district.
(d) When I was a *kid* I went everywhere by *bike.*
(e) My grandfather usually has a *snooze* after lunch.
(f) Did you really find £50, or are you *kidding?*
(g) She lives in just one room and has to share a kitchen, bathroom and *loo* with the other people in the house.
(h) I'm *broke.* Can you lend me some money?
(i) I'm afraid I drank too much and got a bit *merry.*
(j) You can't believe everything you read in the *paper.*
(k) She's very untidy. She leaves her *stuff* lying all over the place.

Popular Language

Popular language is constantly changing, and the best way to keep up-to-date with it is to read popular magazines and watch popular shows etc. in the media. Here are some examples.

-aholic *(suffix)* addicted to something, e.g. chocaholic, workaholic, shopaholic

airhead fool, stupid person

A.OK good, all in order

back off go away, don't bother me

bad-mouth *(v)* to criticise

ball game situation: 'It's a different ball game now.'

belly-ache *(v)* to complain

bent corrupt, e.g. of police or politicians

big deal something special

bimbo attractive, empty-headed young woman

bin it throw it away

boo-boo *(n)* mistake

bottom line basic situation or assessment:'Whatever happens, the bottom line is that if you fail your exams, you won't get a university place.'

brill abbreviation for 'brilliant'

cat's whiskers exceptional, the best: 'She thinks she's the cat's whiskers'.

chill out relax, take it easy

clapped out old, worn-out

cool good, calm

cost an arm and a leg cost a lot of money

couch potato someone who does nothing but stay at home and watch TV

crummy boring, poor quality

damage *(n)* the cost, the bill: 'Let's call the waiter and see what the damage is.'

do the business do the job that has to be done

down to dependent on, due to: 'The success is down to the new manager.'

drop out *(n/v)* give up normal education or work for an unconventional lifestyle

dweeb fool, stupid person

fave abbreviation for 'favourite'

fink dishonest, disloyal person

flavour of the month current fashion or preference, thought to be only temporary

flip *(v)* to react very emotionally or excitedly: 'When I first heard that song, I just flipped.'

-friendly *(suffix)* easily used by, not harmful to, e.g. child-friendly, user-friendly, environment-friendly

fringe *(adj/n)* non-conventional, e.g. fringe theatre, on the fringe, fringe religion/medicine

get a kick out of get satisfaction from

get your act together get organised

give it a whirl try it: 'That new restaurant. Let's give it a whirl.'

give me a break don't keep pestering me/pressurising me/being unreasonable: 'I can't do this in one hour! Give me a break!'

glam abbreviation for 'glamorous'

the glitterati famous people, esp. in literary, arts, entertainment circles

go *(v)* used instead of 'say'/'said': 'He goes, "What are you doing?" And I go,"Nothing."'

gobsmacked *(adj)* shocked, amazed

grotty low quality

gutted *(adj)* very disappointed, devastated: 'I was gutted by the news.'

hang out *(n/v)* place frequented/to frequent

hang-up problem, inhibition

hunk masculine, attractive man

info abbreviation for 'information'

into interested in: 'He's into music/yoga/drugs.'

k thousand, esp. money: 'I was offered 19,000k a year.'

laid back *(adj)* calm, relaxed

legless drunk

the main man most important person

makeover complete transformation (of appearance, character etc.)

mega- *(prefix)* extremely, e.g. mega-rich/famous/store/star

minder celebrity's bodyguard

motor-mouth someone who talks all the time

name of the game the nature of the business, the basic purpose or reason

nerd foolish, boring person

off one's trolley mad, crazy

on the ball alert, efficient

on your bike! Go! Get on with it!

party pooper unsociable person

phoney false, not genuine

play it by ear make decisions depending on what happens: 'Our plans depend on the weather. We'll play everything by ear.'

plus and, in addition

rap *(v/n)* talk

reckon think: 'I reckon it'll rain soon.'

role model an example to others

seriously extremely, e.g. seriously rich, seriously drunk, seriously famous

shoot the breeze chat

sleaze corruption, squalor

state of the art the very best, latest (esp. technology)

straight heterosexual

suit *(n)* respectable person (wearing a suit)

sweat *(n)* hard work: 'Cleaning windows is a real sweat.'
Also: **no sweat**: 'No problem.'

tacky cheap, badly-made, over-sentimental

throw a wobbly to over-react

trash *(v)* to speak contemptuously of

up the creek in trouble

wally a foolish, stupid person

what's with...? What's wrong with...?

wicked excellent, enjoyable

wimp boring, weak person

wind up *(n/v)* irritation or annoyance/to irritate or annoy: 'Are you trying to wind me up?'

you name it the speaker or subject has seen/done etc. everything you can name: 'I've done all kinds of jobs. You name it (and I've done it).'

yuppie *(n/adj)* young urban professional person (and attitudes, lifestyle etc.)

zilch nothing: 'What did you buy in the sales?' 'Zilch - everything was still too expensive.'

IDIOMS FROM SPORTS AND GAMES

Many idioms in general use come from popular sports and games. Can you explain the following?

horse-racing	neck and neck, hot favourite, odds
boxing	low blow, down and out, opening rounds
sailing	to weather the storm, plain sailing
chess	stalemate, checkmate, pawn
cards	put all your cards on the table, poker-face
various	last lap, bull's-eye, set your sights on, kick-off

American Words

1   The American words in the sentences below are printed in italics.
Replace each American word or phrase with a British word or phrase from
the following list.

fail	flat	trousers	playing truant
bill	holidays	nappies	railway timetable
tap	caretaker	pavement	chemist
post	postman	saloon car	ordinary uniformed policeman
rise			

(a) His mother thought he was at school but in fact he was *playing hookey.*
    He'll probably *flunk* his exams.
(b) The kitchen *faucet* in my *apartment* isn't working. I'll tell the *janitor.*
    He'll get it fixed.
(c) Blue-collar workers are asking for a pay-*hike* and longer paid *vacations.*
(d) The dog attacked the *mailman* and tore his *pants.*
(e) Do you have a *railroad schedule*? I want an early train for Chicago tomorrow.
(f) A *patrolman* reported a light-blue *sedan* parked right across the *sidewalk* on
    3rd Street.
(g) She has a little baby so she has to make regular visits to the *drugstore* to buy
    diapers.
(h) When the waiter handed me the *check* after the meal, I found that I had no
    money!
(i) How much does it cost to *mail* a letter to Australia?

2   Instructions as above.

petrol	jam	underground	specialise (university studies)
queue	garden	cinema	maths(mathematics)
rubbish	note	petrol station	secondary school
autumn	lift	ground floor	university
sweets	shops	windscreen	

(a) We had to *stand in line* at the *movie-theater* last night.
(b) Our back *yard* looks lovely in the *fall.* The leaves on the trees turn brown and red.
(c) He wants to *major* in *math* at *college* when he leaves *high school.*
(d) When you stop for *gas* at a *gas station,* they sometimes clean your *windshield.*
(e) We had to buy a lot at the *stores,* then we took the *subway* home.
(f) The *elevator*'s broken down again, but it doesn't matter. We live on the *first floor.*
(g) She likes *candy,* and bread and butter with *jelly* on it. They're bad for her teeth.
(h) The only money I have is a twenty dollar *bill.*
(i) In this district they only collect the *garbage* once a week.

Newspaper Headlines

Vocabulary

1   Certain words are found in newspaper headlines sometimes with a different meaning from that of their normal use. For each of the following 'headline words' on the left, find an item on the right with the same meaning (it will help you if you look at the headlines in exercise 2 below).

(a)	**AXE**	fire
(b)	**BID**	close down, dismiss (usually for economic reasons)
(c)	**BLAST**	conflict, disagree(ment), fight, fighting
(d)	**BLAZE**	diplomat
(e)	**CLASH**	exciting or dramatic event
(f)	**CURB**	attempt
(g)	**DRAMA**	explosion
(h)	**ENVOY**	affect badly
(i)	**HIT**	vote, election, public opinion survey
(j)	**POLL**	reduce, reduction, limit
(k)	**PROBE**	investigate, investigation
(l)	**QUIT**	question, interrogate, interview
(m)	**QUIZ**	reduce drastically
(n)	**RIDDLE**	leave, depart, resign
(o)	**SEEK**	attract, interest, win the support of
(p)	**SLASH**	look for, want, ask for
(q)	**STORM**	mystery
(r)	**TOLL**	marry
(s)	**WED**	angry argument
(t)	**WOO**	total number of dead

2   In headlines, as well as special vocabulary being used, some words (a, the, some, be, been etc.) are often omitted, abbreviations are common, and verb tenses are sometimes used differently. Explain the following headlines in simple English.

e.g. UK TO SEND MORE AID TO GHANA

The United Kingdom is going to send more help to Ghana.

(a) **ARMY AXES 3 BASES, 3,000 MEN**
(b) **BID TO REACH NORTH POLE FAILS**
(c) **HOTEL BLAST KILLS 8**
(d) **ANIMALS DIE IN ZOO BLAZE**
(e) **US, RUSSIA CLASH OVER ARMS CURBS**
(f) **3 SAVED IN FLATS BLAZE DRAMA**
(g) **ENVOY ACCUSED OF SPYING**
(h) **TOURISTS HIT BY PILOTS' STRIKE**
(i) **PM ANNOUNCES MARCH POLL**
(j) **POLICE PROBE MISSING WOMAN RIDDLE**
(k) **TOP SCIENTIST QUITS UK FOR US**
(l) **3 QUIZZED OVER BOY'S KIDNAP**
(m) **FILM STAR SEEKS DIVORCE**
(n) **AIR FARES SLASHED TO WOO HOLIDAY MAKERS**
(o) **STORM AT UN OVER 'SPIES' ACCUSATION**
(p) **EARTHQUAKE TOLL REACHES 27**
(q) **ACTOR TO WED FOR FIFTH TIME**

Abbreviations

Abbreviations are a common part of language. We use many of them in spoken English, pronouncing them either as initials (BBC, EU, FBI) or sometimes as complete words in themselves (NATO, OPEC).

Some abbreviations are used only in the written form (Bros. St. Esq) and other abbreviations represent the original Latin or occasionally French or Italian words and are spoken quite differently from their written form (lb. oz).

1   Put each of the following abbreviations in its correct place in the sentences below. The full version of each abbreviation is given at the end of the exercise.

NSPCC	AA	BBC	C of E	ITV	BA	BR	M4	Esq
RSPCA	in	M15	OHMS	oz	c/o	ft	lb	Rd

(a)   Non-commercial radio and television in Britain is controlled by the _____ .

(b)   The _____ investigates cases of cruelty to children.

(c)   The _____ protects and cares for animals.

(d)   The _____ is the biggest organisation for motorists in Britain.

(e)   If asked which church they belonged to, most English people would say

_____ .

(f)   _____ is the main British state security organisation, responsible for acting against foreign espionage.

(g)   _____ operates the railways system in Britain.

(h)   Letters from government offices usually have the initials _____ on the envelopes.

(i)   The first degree in an arts subject from a British university is the _____ .

(j)   The _____ runs from London to the south-west of England.

(k)   Most people enjoy watching the commercials (advertisements) between _____ programmes.

(l)   The weight of the parcel was 3 _____ 10 _____ .

(m) The length of the room is 22 _____ 6 _____ .

(n)   John M Carter _____ , _____ Mr and Mrs R. Waters, 21, Feltham _____ , London SW6.

Automobile Association
Bachelor of Arts
British Broadcasting Corporation
Church of England
foot/feet (1 ft = 0.3048 m)
Independent Television
Military Intelligence Department No 5
On Her Majesty's Service
Esquire (formal title for a man used in addresses)
National Society for the Prevention of Cruelty to Children
Royal Society for the Prevention of Cruelty to Animals.

care of
British Rail
inch(es) (1 in = 2.54 cm)
Motorway No 4
ounce(s) (1 oz = 28.35 g)
Road
pound(s) (lb = 0.454 kg)

2 Instructions as above

CIA   FBI   OPEC   UK   US   EU   NATO   UN

(a)   The _____ was set up in 1945 to keep world peace and help international co-operation.

(b)   The modern _____ grew out of the original European Community, also known as the Common Market.

(c)   Most countries which export oil belong to _____ .

(d)   The American _____ works, normally secretly, to collect information about other countries.

(e)   _____ is a military alliance of the USA, Canada, and most West European countries, Greece and Turkey.

(f)   The _____ investigates crime in America.

(g)   There are fifty states in the _____ .

(h)   The _____ consists of Great Britain (England, Scotland, Wales, the Channel Islands and the Isle of Man) and Northern Ireland.

Central Intelligence Agency	Organisation of Petroleum Exporting Countries
European Union	United Kingdom
Federal Bureau of Investigation	United Nations
North Atlantic Treaty Organisation	United States (of America)

3   Instructions as above.

AD   CD   PTO   °F   PS   St   PIN   vs   BC   Bros   °C   RSVP   No

(a)   I didn't know anything was written on the other side of the page. Why didn't you write _____ at the bottom?

(b)   INTERNATIONAL FOOTBALL. ITALY _____ SPAIN.

(c)   The address of the firm was written as, 'Johnson _____ , 82 East Dock _____ , London E5.'

(d)   The Roman general, Julius Caesar, came to Britain over 2,000 years ago in 55 _____ .

(e)   The summer temperature in Britain rises to about 80 _____ , that's about 27 _____ .

(f)   That house is more than 100 years old. It has '_____ 1877' on the wall.

(g)   The wedding invitation had _____ written on it, so I replied at once.

(h)   After finishing the letter to his parents, he thought for a moment and then added '_____ Please send more money.'

(i)   Exam candidates must answer question _____1 and any two others.

(j)   Most people think a _____ gives better sound quality than a cassette.

(k)   To get money from an automatic cash dispenser, you'll need your cash card and your _____.

Anno Domini (in the year of our Lord)	Please Turn Over
Compact disc	Postscript
Before Christ	Respondez s'il vous plaît (please reply)
Brothers	Street
degrees Celsius or centigrade	Personal Identification Number
degrees Fahrenheit	versus (against)
Number	

Classified Advertisements

In these exercises find a word, phrase or abbreviation in the advertisements to fit each explanation below it.

1   FLATS TO LET

W. London, single bed-sit to let, suit stdnt, own ckng-facilities, share b&w.c.£55 wkly. inc. g/elec. 0171 248 4563 after 7.	**Cent. London. Self-contained, fully-furn. c.h., 2 beds, lounge, labour-saving kit. b/w.c., handy tube £800 p.m. 0171 266 4792**

(a)   one all-purpose room for sleeping, studying, relaxing
(b)   a simple cooker and perhaps a sink and refrigerator
(c)   available for renting
(d)   centrally heated
(e)   all furniture provided
(f)   bathroom with a toilet in it
(g)   no extra charges for lighting, heating etc.
(h)   with modern equipment so you don't have to do much manually
(i)   has all necessary facilities so you don't need to share anything
(j)   conveniently near an underground station
(k)   sitting room, living room
(l)   it would suit (be suitable for)

2   VACANCIES

Sales manager frozen food co. £24,000 p.a. negotiable, ann. increments, commission, gd. fringe benefits, gd. prospects, send c.v. & references to Icepro. 8 Port St., Plymouth, Devon.	Department Store assistants, m/f, 17+, £10,000 p.a., shopping discount, pens scheme, ann. bonus, gd. pos. for sch. leavers, apply for interview Barons, George St. Plymouth, Devon.

(a)   men or women, boys or girls
(b)   an extra payment to all employees every year
(c)   employees will receive a pension when they retire
(d)   you will receive a percentage of all the goods you sell
(e)   summary of your education, qualifications, jobs
(f)   automatic increase of salary every year
(g)   annually, every year
(h)   letters from previous employers describing your ability and experience
(i)   employees can buy goods at reduced prices
(j)   other advantages are offered besides basic pay and conditions (car, subsidised meals, health insurance etc.)
(k)   the salary can be discussed and might be more than advertised
(l)   there is a good opportunity to improve your position
(m)   at least, or more

3   HOLIDAYS

Fortnight in Spain £400 all-inclusive gd. hotel, air travel, insur. full-board, send s.a.e. for brochure, Iberiahols, 1 Nash Way, Brighton, Sussex.	Off-peak hols., self-catering villas or hotels (half-board) in France. B&b in Malta. Deps from all major UK airports. Also fabulous fly/drive deals. Medsun 01583 2456.	Greece overland, minibus, expd. drvr/guide cmpng, 3 weeks, £200 excl. food Venturetours 01491 8873.

(a)   combined return air-fares and car-hire
(b)   doing your own shopping and cooking
(c)   sleeping in tents
(d)   accommodation and breakfast
(e)   breakfast and dinner will be provided, not lunch
(f)   all meals will be provided
(g)   an envelope, stamped and with your own address on it
(h)   the price covers everything
(i)   travelling by road, not air
(j)   outside the main, most popular season

4   MISCELLANEOUS

House painting, free estimate, all work fully gurntd, refs. available, Watson 01621 8407	Gent's sec hnd bike, all accessories (lights, tools), gd. cond. £30 0181 933 2722	Ford Sierra 87, red, leather upholstery, good m.p.g., low mileage, ex. cond. £4,000 o.n.o. 01941 8731 weekdays.	Ex-demonstration, shop-soiled gas cooker, £150, v.g.c., byr to collect, Gastore, High St., Rill, Essex.

(a)   used, not new
(b)   seat material
(c)   man's
(d)   extra attachments
(e)   Mondays to Fridays
(f)   has not been driven very much
(g)   fuel consumption (distance car will go on one gallon of petrol)
(h)   has been used to show people how it works
(i)   you will be told, without charge, the cost of the work first
(j)   you can look at letters from satisfied customers
(k)   the seller might accept a lower price
(l)   if the work isn't done well enough, we promise to put it right
(m)   has been on display, so is not in completely clean condition
(n)   seller will not deliver, so you must arrange transport

Write your own advertisement for
(a)   a room or flat to let.
(b)   your job, or one you would like.
(c)   a holiday you would enjoy.
(d)   something you want to sell or a service you can offer.

Shortened Words

1   Some common words are best known and more often used in their abbreviated form (often with a small change in spelling), e.g. 'fridge' instead of 'refrigerator'. Give the short forms of the following.

photograph	telephone	popular (music)
mackintosh	aeroplane	public house
motor-cycle	motor-car	zoological gardens
gymnasium	taxi-cab	examination
newspaper	bicycle	veterinary surgeon
hippopotamus	kilogram	facsimile transmission

2   Other words are normally used in their full form, but are sometimes shortened in conversational, colloquial use, e.g. 'hankie' for 'handkerchief'. Give the full form of each word below.

ad, advert	lab	comfy
limo	doc	(women's) lib
nightie	mike	champ (sport)
demo	specs	pro (sport)

Problem Pairs

Pairs of Words Often Confused

Choose the correct word for each space below.

1   lose/loose
(a) Look after that money or you'll _____ it.
(b) That screw is a bit _____ . You'd better tighten it.
(c) The opposite of 'to find' is 'to _____ '.
(d) I tied the dog to a tree but it got _____ and ran away.

2   their/there
(a) The students brought _____ books.
(b) They are having _____ breakfast.
(c) _____ are my friends!
(d) It's a nice place. I often go _____ .

3   advice/advise
(a) I _____ you to see a doctor.
(b) She didn't listen to her father's _____ .
(c) I'm very grateful to you for your _____ .
(d) I really don't know what to _____ .

4   weather/whether
(a) I don't know _____ to see that film or not.
(b) Their holiday was spoilt by bad _____ .
(c) What's the _____ like? Is it sunny?
(d) She can't decide _____ she ought to marry him.

5   beside/besides
(a) The post office is _____ the cinema.
(b) They always sit _____ each other in class.
(c) There are several big parks in London _____ Hyde Park.
(d) What languages does he speak _____ Swedish?

6   stationery/stationary
(a) The bus stood _____ in the traffic jam for 20 minutes.
(b) The teacher got some paper from the school _____ cupboard.
(c) The weather system over Western Europe has been _____ for two days.
(d) The office staff were told to use paper more carefully, since the _____ bill the month before had been very high.

7   accept/agree
(a) He thinks she's beautiful but I don't _____ with him.
(b) This machine does not _____ damaged coins.
(c) They will only _____ to do the job if you pay them first.
(d) He cannot _____ the fact that his wife is dead.

8   comprehensive/understanding

(a) A priest is normally a patient, _____ person.
(b) It's a very _____ book. It covers all aspects of the subject.
(c) London taxi drivers have a very _____ knowledge of the city.
(d) Whatever stupid things he did, his mother was always _____ and she forgave him.

9   sensible/sensitive

(a) It's _____ to save part of your salary every month.
(b) Don't laugh at him. He's very _____ about his appearance.
(c) It's cold. I think it would be _____ to take a warm coat with you.
(d) My skin is very _____ to the sun. Film is _____ to light.

10   actually/now

(a) Ten years ago he had nothing; _____ he is a millionaire.
(b) I've lost contact with him. I don't know where he is _____ .
(c) Is that necklace _____ made of gold?
(d) Tell me the truth. What _____ happened?

11   control/check

(a) The police were unable to _____ the football fans, who ran on to the pitch fighting and shouting.
(b) An inspector came along the train to _____ all the tickets.
(c) He's really a wild boy. His parents can't _____ him.
(d) I advise you to _____ all your exam answers before you hand your paper in.

12   teacher/professor

(a) The _____ told his class to do their homework carefully.
(b) When I was at school I had a very good history _____ .
(c) He taught at the university for many years but he never became a _____ .
(d) _____ Bolton is head of the Chemistry Faculty at the University of York.

13   affect/effect

(a) The punishment had no _____ on him. As soon as he left prison he began to steal again.
(b) The new taxes will _____ the rich, they'll have to pay more.
(c) The higher bus fares won't _____ me. I have a car.
(d) The medicine had an immediate _____ . I felt better at once.

14   past/passed

(a) I've _____ the exam!
(b) She _____ the post office on her way home, but forgot to go in.
(c) The thief hid in a doorway and the policeman ran _____ him.
(d) It was _____ midnight when I finally got to bed.

15   economic/economical

(a) It isn't very _____ to leave the lights on when you're not in the room.
(b) Because of the recent strikes, the _____ situation of the country is very bad.
(c) She's an economist. She's an expert in _____ matters.
(d) It's a very _____ little car. It uses very little petrol.

16 principal/principle(s)
(a) Telling lies is against his _____ .
(b) He believed in the _____ that all men are equal.
(c) Mr Williams is the _____ of this college.
(d) Oxford Street is one of the _____ shopping streets of London.

17 grateful/thankful
(a) I'm very _____ to you for your help.
(b) He was very ashamed of what he had done and was _____ that his family didn't know about it.
(c) We were all _____ that the weather was good for the picnic.
(d) She was very _____ to her parents for their advice and support.

18 lend/borrow
(a) Can you _____ me some money till Monday?
(b) Ireland had to _____ some money from the World Bank.
(c) We _____ books from the library.
(d) I'll _____ you my car if you promise to drive carefully.

19 quite/quiet
(a) It's noisy here. Let's find a _____ place.
(b) I'm _____ satisfied, thank you.
(c) Sometimes she longed for the peace and _____ of the country.
(d) He hadn't _____ finished when I came in.

20 canal(s)/channel
(a) The shortest sea-route from Europe to India is through the Suez _____ .
(b) Before railways the _____ between cities were important routes of transport.
(c) The seaway between Britain and France is often called the English _____ .
(d) He was bored by the television programme so he changed to a different _____ .

21 priceless/valueless
(a) The painting turned out to be _____ , so I threw it away
(b) The Crown Jewels of the Royal Family cannot be insured. They are _____ .
(c) The contents of the Uffizi Gallery in Florence are, of course, _____ . They are of incalculable value.
(d) Although these stamps are _____ , I like them for their colour and design.

22 invaluable/worthless
(a) A cassette-recorder is _____ in a pronunciation class.
(b) Thank you so much for your advice. It was _____ .
(c) The information was completely false, quite _____ .
(d) These bank notes are no longer in use. I'm afraid they're _____ .

23 continuously/continually
(a) She is _____ coming late!
(b) It rained _____ for three hours this morning.
(c) The firemen worked _____ through the night to put out the flames.
(d) I'm afraid you _____ make the same mistakes in your work.

24 hard/hardly

(a) She's a _____ worker.

(b) She works very _____ .

(c) I was so tired I could _____ speak.

(d) He had _____ got home when the phone rang.

25 avoid/prevent

(a) I try to _____ travelling in the rush hour. It's so tiring.

(b) The police managed to _____ the crowd from moving forward.

(c) We must do something to _____ such a thing happening again.

(d) He swerved to the left to _____ the car coming towards him.

26 rise rose risen/raise raised raised

e.g. Taxes will rise.
The sun rises in the east.
He raised his hat.
Their hopes are rising.

When the President entered, everyone rose.
Prices will be raised by many shopkeepers.
Raise your hand if you have a question.

Choose the correct verb in each sentence below.

(a) They (rose/raised) their glasses and drank to the happy couple.

(b) Of course prices always (rise/raise) in a time of inflation.

(c) The smoke (rose/raised) high into the air.

(d) College fees will be (risen/raised) from next September.

(e) The two parts of Tower Bridge (rise/raise) to allow ships to go through.

(f) The two parts of the bridge are (risen/raised) by very powerful machinery.

(g) She couldn't hear him so he (rose/raised) his voice.

(h) The water level has (risen/raised) six inches in the last three days.

(i) The number of deaths in traffic accidents (rises/raises) every year.

(j) He (rose/raised) his head and looked at her.

27 steal stole stolen/rob robbed robbed

e.g. Someone stole £10 from her.
£10 was stolen from her.

A gang robbed the bank of £10,000.
The bank was robbed of £10,000.

Choose the correct verb in each sentence below.

(a) He (stole/robbed) a bottle of whisky from the shop.

(b) He was stopped and (stolen/robbed) by two armed men.

(c) Two banks were (stolen/robbed) last week.

(d) If you leave your money there, it'll be (stolen/robbed).

(e) Someone's (stolen/robbed) my wallet!

(f) They were planning to (steal/rob) a shop.

(g) She (stole/robbed) some clothes from her employers.

(h) We've been (stolen/robbed). Look, all our silver's gone!

(i) In the old days they used to hang people who (stole/robbed) sheep.

28 lie lay lain/lay laid laid

e.g. Switzerland lies in central Europe.
He lay down on the grass.
His clothes were lying on the floor.
It had lain hidden for centuries.

Lay the books on the table.
He laid his hand on my shoulder.
The hen has laid an egg.
The bricks were laid badly.

Choose the correct verb in each sentence below.

(a)   Liverpool (lies/lays) on the north bank of the River Mersey estuary.
(b)   She gave the baby a kiss and (lay/laid) it on the bed.
(c)   Hurry up! (Lie/Lay) the table!
(d)   The dogs entered the room and (lay/laid) down near the fire.
(e)   He had (lain/laid) on the pavement for twenty minutes before help came.
(f)   He ordered the dog to (lie/lay) the newspaper at his feet.
(g)   He ordered the dog to (lie/lay) down.
(h)   This table has been carelessly (lain/laid).
(i)   All his belongings were (lying/laying) in a mess on the floor.
(j)   The porter had to (lie/lay) the luggage down and take a breath.
(k)   The Mayor (lay/laid) the foundation stone of this building in 1965.
(l)   The soldiers ordered the terrorists to (lie/lay) down their arms, and then to
(lie/lay) down on the ground with their hands behind their backs.

29 remember/remind

e.g. I remember meeting you in Paris.
You remind me of my brother.
Sorry, I can't remember your name.
I hope he remembers to phone me.

Please remind me to post this letter.
Please remember to turn off the lights.
I must remind you that the exam is today.
Did you remind her about our meeting?

Choose the correct verb in each sentence below.

(a)   What's Sandra's phone number? I can't (remember/remind).
(b)   Some parts of the city (remember/remind) me of my home town.
(c)   I must (remember/remind) to get some stamps from the post office today.
(d)   I (remember/remind) coming here when I was a child.
(e)   She (remembered/reminded) the class to be at the station early for the trip to
the seaside.
(f)   He's very forgetful. His children always have to (remember/remind) him about
his wife's birthday.
(g)   Please (remember/remind) that the ABC Company is our most important customer.
(h)   I have to (remember/remind) you that our business with the ABC Company is
very important to us.
(i)   Do you (remember/remind) if I locked the door when we left the house?
(j)   There's John! Oh, that (remembers/reminds) me! He owes me some money.

One Word or Two?

Choose the correct word or two-word phrase to put in the sentences which follow each pair of expressions.

maybe   may be

(a)   I don't know where he is. He _____ at the shops.
(b)   I don't know where he is. _____ he's at the shops.

alright   all right

(c)   How are you? Are you _____?
(d)   The exam questions were easy. She got them _____.

altogether   all together

(e)   There were three adults and five children. That's eight people _____.
(f)   Shall we go there separately or shall we go _____?

sometimes   some times

(g)   At _____ in the year the hotel is full.
(h)   _____ the hotel is full.

already   all ready

(i)   Have you finished _____?
(j)   The children were _____ to leave.

everyone   every one

(k)   _____ came to the party with a present for Jim.
(l)   He has 28 shirts, and _____ is hand-made.

anyone   any one

(m) Has _____ got a pen to lend me?
(n)   They have 75 nuclear bombs and _____ of them has the power to destroy an entire city.

nobody   no body

(o)   Despite an intensive hunt for the murder victim, _____ was ever found.
(p)   _____ admitted responsibility for the crime.

everyday   every day

(q)   There's no need to dress up specially. Just wear your _____ clothes.
(r)   He goes to the office by train _____.

Spelling Rules

Noun plurals

	singular	plural	points
final -s -ss, -ch, -sh, -x	bus, loss, church, brush, box	buses, losses, churches, brushes, boxes	add -es exception: loch-lochs
final -y	boy, donkey, tray, valley	boys, donkeys, trays, valleys	add -s if -y follows vowel
	fly, lady, body, lorry	flies, ladies, bodies, lorries	drop -y and add -ies if -y follows consonant
	Kennedy, Mary	Kennedys, Marys	exception: proper nouns
final -f, -fe	knife, loaf, shelf, self, half, thief, life, wolf, calf, leaf, wife	knives, loaves, shelves, selves, halves, thieves, lives, wolves, calves, leaves, wives	certain nouns drop -f, -fe and add -ves
	roof, chief, reef, safe, handkerchief, cliff	roofs, chiefs, reefs, safes, handkerchiefs, cliffs	others add -s
	hoof, wharf, scarf	hoofs/hooves, wharfs/wharves, scarfs/scarves	some have alternative endings
final -o	photo, memo, kilo, piano, cello, solo, radio, video, zoo, Eskimo Filipino	photos, memos, kilos, pianos, cellos, solos, radios, videos, zoos, Eskimos, Filipinos	most nouns add -s
	tomato, echo, hero, cargo, volcano	tomatoes, echoes, heroes, cargoes, volcanoes	but some very common nouns add -es
	banjo, zero, mosquito	banjos/banjoes, zeros/zeroes, mosquitos/mosquitoes	some have alternative endings
irregular	child, tooth, goose, foot, man, woman, mouse	children, teeth, geese, feet, men, women, mice	
nouns of foreign origin	criterion, medium, crisis, chateau, bureau,	criteria, media, crises, chateaux, bureaux	some keep original plural ending
	aquarium, stadium, gymnasium	aquariums, stadiums, gymnasiums	some have become anglicized
	fungus, formula, curriculum	fungi/funguses, formulae/formulas, curriculi/curriculums	some have alternative endings
no change	aircraft, sheep, deer, fish	aircraft, sheep, deer, fish*	no change (but these are not uncountable nouns)
compound nouns	tooth-brush, city centre, concert-hall	tooth-brushes, city centres, concert-halls	true noun normally becomes plural, noun-used-as-adjective does not change
	commander-in-chief, passer-by, son-in-law	commanders-in-chief, passers-by, sons-in-law	
	court-martial	courts-martial, court-marshals	some have alternative endings

*the plural form 'fishes' is sometimes used.

-ing form and regular -ed past tense form of one-syllable verbs

verbs	points	-ing form	regular -ed form
wait, help be, shoot	most verbs just add -ing/-ed	waiting, helping, being, shooting	waited, helped
stop, ban, sit, swim	final single consonant after one vowel doubles	stopping, banning, sitting, swimming	stopped, banned
buy, blow, box	exception: -y, -w, -x, never double	buying, blowing, boxing	boxed
write, care, hope, come	final single -e after consonant is dropped	writing, caring, hoping, coming	cared hoped
lie, die, tie	final -ie replaced with -y	lying, dying tying	

-ing form and regular -ed past tense form of two-syllable verbs ending in one consonant after one vowel

verbs	stress	points	-ing form	regular -ed form
'listen, 'answer, 'visit, 'murmur	first syllable	just add -ing/-ed	listening, answering, visiting, murmuring	listened, answered, visited, murmured
'travel, 'cancel,		exceptions: -l always doubles	travelling, cancelling	travelled, cancelled
'picnic, 'panic,		add -k	picnicking, panicking	picnicked, panicked
'kidnap, 'worship 'gossip, 'gallop		-p sometimes doubles	kidnapping, worshipping, gossiping, galloping	kidnapped, worshipped, gossiped, galloped
be'gin, re'fer, re'gret, o'ccur	second syllable	final consonant doubles	beginning, referring, regretting, occurring	referred, regretted, occurred
a'llow, con'vey		exception: -w, -y, -x, never double	allowing, conveying	allowed, conveyed

General Spelling Points

words	points
brief ceiling believe receive piece deceive	-i before -e except after -c, but only where the -ie or -ei is pronounced /i:/ as in seen main exception: seize
responsible telephone independent	don't confuse with similar words in other languages
fought thought wrought caught brought sought bought taught	many verbs have past form ought but note: catch – caught teach – taught (same sound)
basic – basically tragic – tragically rustic – rustically heroic – heroically	adjectives ending -ic add -ally for adverb main exception: publicly
lazy – lazier, laziest, lazily, laziness happy – happier, happiest, happily, happiness beauty – beautiful copy – copier	final -y after a consonant changes to -i before -er, -est, -ness, -ly, -ful some exceptions e.g. dry drier or dryer
careful useful painful beautiful awful carefully usefully painfully beautifully awfully	-ful as a suffix: one -l but adverb form: double -l
mystery system physical hymn symphony pyramid rhythm sympathy myth gymnasium	/ɪ/ sound (as in 'sit') is often spelt with -y
advise – advice prophesy – prophecy license – licence devise – device practise – practice	some words take -s in verb form, -c in noun
whose – who's principal – principle lose – loose its – it's weather – whether quite – quiet passed – past stationery – stationary minor – miner there – their dependent – dependant break – brake your – you're envelope – envelop born – borne	be careful of pairs of words with the same or similar pronunciation
almost, also, already, alright, although, altogether, always	al- as a prefix: one -l
miscellaneous knee scissors character guess exhausted knife spaghetti scene solemn exhibition school honest comb acquire psychological guard rhythm hour wrong acquaintance debt receipt autumn column	note the silent letters in these words
accommodation committee address commit occasion Mediterranean excellent different parallel immediate exaggerate professor success necessary possess marvellous tobacco immigrate embarrass opportunity recommend coffee connect possible abbreviate	note the double consonants

Principal British-American Spelling Differences

British	American	British	American
aeroplane	airplane	metre	meter
aluminium	aluminum	neighbour	neighbor
analyse	analyze	offence	offense
axe	ax	plough	plow
catalogue	catalog	practise	practice
centre	center	pretence	pretense
cheque	check	programme*	program
colour	color	pyjamas	pajamas
defence	defense	quarrel-ling, -ler, -led	quarrel-ing, -er, -ed
dialogue	dialog	skilful	skillful
favourite	favorite	storey	story
grey	gray	theatre	theater
humour	humor	travel-ling, -ler, led	travel-ing, -er, -ed
jewellery	jewelry	tyre	tire
kidnap-ping, -per, -ped	kidnap-ing, -er, -ed	worship-ping -ped, -per	worship-ing -ed, -er
labour	labor		
licence	license		

* British spelling is also 'program' for a computer program.

PROVERBS

Proverbs are often used in jokes, advertisements and ordinary conversation.
Do you understand these?

Any port in a storm.
All's fair in love and war.
Beggars can't be choosers.
Love is blind.
Let bygones be bygones.
Better late than never.
Troubles never come singly.
Look before you leap.

All that glitters is not gold.
A leopard can't change his spots.
All's well that ends well.
He who hesitates is lost.
The end justifies the means.
Two heads are better than one.
One good turn deserves another.
Make hay while the sun shines.

Word Games

1   Make as many words as you can from *Great Britain*. Each letter can be used only once in each new word. Words must contain four letters or more. No proper nouns are allowed. Then try again with *accidental* and *unfortunately*.

2   How many pairs of words can you make which are the reverse of each other in spelling? e.g. raw-war, part-trap

3   Make words from each of the following combinations of letters, using the letters in the same order.

    e.g. *TRR - straighter, terrible*
          LPD - slipped, limped
          CTN   SLR   LWR   BNS   EVS   FTN   OLG

4   In a word square, like those below, the words read the same left to right and top to bottom. Can you make your own 9 or 16-letter square?

F	A	T
A	I	R
T	R	Y

C	O	M	E
O	V	A	L
M	A	S	S
E	L	S	E

5   Rearrange the letters in the words on the right to form examples of the categories given in brackets,

    e.g. animal *shore*   Answer: horse

occupations	treprance	rotac	yerwal	roflabotle
	mailponce	drooct	creathe	olicipiant
countries	gratanine	imblegu	geraila	dannawezel
	odaninise	vilabio	danngle	acoshifarut
clothing	wendaurer	wastree	acration	volerulp
	octavero	souble	rortessu	caktej

6   You can probably find crosswords to do, but can you make up your own from this?

CLUES

Across	Down
1	1
4	2
6	3
8	5
9	7

7 For each word below give another which has a different spelling and meaning but **exactly the same pronunciation**.

e.g. road – rode   patience – patients

mist	break	size	weak	see	flower
bear	sight	isle	pain	saw	prints

8 Rearrange the nonsense compound nouns in each group below so that they make seven real compound nouns.

(a)

```
E G G   M A T
B A C K   B A N K
L I G H T   M O N E Y
P O C K E T   O P E N E R
R I V E R   H O U S E
D O O R   B O N E
T I N   C U P
```

(b)

```
T E A   B E D
F I R E   H A N D
P A P E R   P A S T E
S P O R T S   E N G I N E
T O O T H   S P O O N
H O U R   C L I P
S E A   C A R
```

9 From each word below make a completely new word (no plurals or past tenses) by adding **one** letter.

e.g. red – re<u>a</u>d   ill – <u>w</u>ill   man – man<u>y</u>

bee	car	back	care	mile	plan
low	sick	ear	end	hot	cat
right	he	eat	were	wear	net

10 In each of the following sentences one letter has been omitted throughout. Put it back and make the original sentence.

e.g. *MBOSPLAWITHTOSEVERDA*

Answer: My boys play with toys every day. (*-y* omitted)

GRNDMLWYSHDBDBCK
THNKLLHTHMFHESSLLYAGAN
HEYHINKISBEEROAKEARAIN
HEAYHEAWOMEONETEALOMECIOR
NLYNERTWBYSKNWWHWRTETHENTE
THTHRVRYWLLDRSSDWOMNWNTTHRVRYWDNSDAY

11 For each pair of words below give another word which has the same meaning as both words.

e.g. volume/reserve <u>book</u>   now/gift <u>present</u>

(a) world/soil
(b) not left/correct
(c) company/stable
(d) piece/separate
(e) worried/eager
(f) type/helpful
(g) insect/go by air
(h) rear/support
(i) let in/confess
(j) strange/amusing

(k) busy/to be married
(l) put on trial/attempt
(m) expensive/beloved
(n) only/part of foot
(o) secure/strong-box
(p) strange/inquisitive
(q) depart/permission
(r) light-coloured/just
(s) write name/notice
(t) annoyed/traverse

Key

Dictionary Practice (p.1–3)

Pronunciation

1 /ʊ/ wood, good, look, book, foot, /u:/ school, food, soon, / ʌ / flood, blood **2** / ɜ:/ first, world, learn, turn, word, /a:/ laugh, heart, fast, hard, calm, / ɔ:/ warm, court, taught, sort, lord **3** (a) self, wolf (b) follow, show (c) union, university (d) chemical, character (e) happy, catastrophe (f) system, mystery (g) rough, tough (h) receive, seize,

Stress

'coffee, pay'ee, 'visit, for'get, em'ployer, employ'ee, 'advertise, ad'vertisement, 'modern, mod'ernity, moderni'sation, a'ttention, ad'mire, 'admirable, admir'ation, 'infamous

Spelling

1 teenager, calendar, survivor, author, soldier, vendor, equator, lecturer, muscular, speaker, burglar, waiter, traitor, nuclear, dollar **2 ei/ie:** piece, ceiling, receive, priest, relief, deceive, niece, seize, weigh, foreign, **ance/ence:** appearance, innocence, correspondence, acquaintance, guidance, violence, insurance, adolescence, occurrence, alliance

Meaning

1 seats: sofa, bench, throne, stool, pew **on the floor:** carpet, parquet, rug, lino **clothing materials:** tweed, denim, velvet, suede, corduroy, silk **metals:** iron, steel, lead, tin, copper, gold **2** hangar-aircraft, holster-revolver, dustbin-rubbish, hearse–coffin, reservoir-water, grandstand-spectators

Word Parts

1 potatoes, theses, strata, chateaux, deer, thieves, crises, sheep, shelves, phenomena
2 foot-sore, footsteps, dogsbody, dog-tired, seasick, seaweed

Word Use

1 (a) is (b) are (c) is (d) is (e) are (f) is (g) is (h) are **2** She discouraged them from going there. I pleaded with her to help me. We succeeded in finishing in time. They prevented him from leaving.

Topics

Air Travel (p.4)

1 (a) check in (b) trolley (c) check-in desk (d) check (e) excess baggage (f) conveyor belt (g) hand luggage (h) immigration officer (i) security guard (j) departure lounge (k) duty free (l) departures board (m) announcement (n) board (o) departure gate (p) security check (q) passengers (r) on board (s) taxi (t) runway (u) take off **2** (a) airliner (b) cabin crew (c) aisle (d) turbulence (e) seat belts (f) headphones (g) land **3** (a) by (b) off (c) through (d) at (e) to … off (f) in (g) on (h) at

Bank Accounts (pp.5-6)

1 (a) open (b) account (c) formalities (d) branch (e) fill in (f) bank charges (g) overdraft **2** (a) current (b) interest (c) cheque (d) deposit (e) withdraw (f) notice **3** (a) statement (b) deposit (c) withdrawal (d) balance (e) standing order **4** (a) expenditure (b) income (c) overdrawn (d) keep a record (e) counterfoil (f) crossed (g) cash **5** (a) from (b) in (c) for (d) to (e) at (f) out of (g) from

Trade Names (p.6)

Snack bar: Mr Sam Widge, **Stationers:** Just Write, **Shoe-repairers:** Nu-a-gane, **Bed shop:** Sleepeezee, **Dry cleaners:** Kwik Kleen, **Travel agency:** Rite Flite

Books and Reading (p.7)

1 (a) atlas (b) textbook (c) dictionary (d) encyclopaedia (e) thriller (f) manual (g) guidebook (h) Who's Who **2** (a) bookworm (b) browse (c) illustrations (d) glossary (e) footnotes (f) bibliography (g) borrow (h) fine (i) reviews (j) published **3** (a) Contents page: normally at the front, tells you what the book contains, in order of chapters or pages. Index: in alphabetical order and usually at the back, a list of names, places etc. mentioned in the book with page references. (b) A bookshop sells books; a library lends them. (c) An author writes books; a publisher prints and sells them. (d) You lend something to someone, and borrow from someone. (e) A biography: someone's life story. An autobiography; a biography written by its subject. (f) Fiction: imaginary writing. Non-fiction: factual writing. Reference books: information books. **4** (a) from (b) at (c) at (d) in (e) up … in (f) by (g) on

Cars (p.8)

1 (a) boot (b) aerial (c) windscreen (d) bonnet (e) bumper (f) number plate (g) headlights (h) tyre (i) engine (j) windscreen wipers (k) wheel (l) exhaust pipe (m) gear lever (n) rear-view mirror (o) dashboard (p) steering wheel (q) seat belt (r) accelerator (pedal) (s) headrest (t) brake (pedal) (u) clutch (pedal) **2** (a) fuel consumption … mpg … petrol tank (b) performance (c) vehicle … rear (d) instruments (e) overtake (f) reverse (g) body (h) indicate

Cinema and Films (p.9)

1 (a) cinema (b) review (c) critic (d) performance (e) foyer (f) poster (g) auditorium (h) screen (i) row (j) aisle (k) cartoon (l) trailer (m) horror **2** (a) performance (b) role (c) cast (d) director (e) studio (f) location (g) documentary (h) critical (i) box office (j) plot **3** (a) on (b) in (c) on (d) on at (e) on (f) at (g) for (h) to (i) on (j) at (k) at (l) to … in (m) at

Doctors and Hospitals (p.10)

1 (a) general practitioner (b) nurse (c) psychiatrist (d) patient (e) in-patient (f) out-patient (g) surgeon (h) casualty (i) midwife (j) medical student (k) specialist **2** (a) receptionist (b) waiting room (c) appointment (d) symptoms (e) examine (f) stethoscope (g) pulse (h) temperature (i) thermometer (j) prescription (k) chemist (l) treatment (m) ward (n) operation **3** (a) on (b) to (c) from (d) in (e) with (f) of (g) for

Education (p.11)

1 (a) nursery school (b) primary (c) academic (d) terms (e) break up (f) secondary (g) co-educational (h) compulsory (i) state (j) private (k) graduate (l) degree (m) tutorial (n) seminar (o) lecture (p) grant (q) fees **2** (a) Students sit an exam. Examiners set an exam. (b) Take an exam: attempt the questions. pass an exam: be successful. (c) Compulsory: required by law or regulation. Voluntary: performed by free choice. (d) Schools and universities educate people. Parents bring them up. (e) A pupil: a child at school. A student: normally an older person and at college or university. **3** (a) to (b) at … of (c) in (d) at (e) to (f) into (g) up (h) at (i) in (j) from (k) by

Elections and Government (p.12)

1 (a) predict (b) opinion poll (c) election campaign (d) support (e) vote (f) polling station (g) polling day (h) ballot box (i) candidate **2** (a) one-party states (b) majority (c) opposition (d) coalition (e) cabinet (f) prime minister (g) left-wing (h) right-wing (i) split (j) alliance **3** (a) Pro-: for, in support of. Anti-: against. (b) An election: when people vote for a person or persons to represent them. A referendum: when a nation votes on one particular issue. **4** (a) for (b) in (c) against (d) to (e) with (f) between (g) in

Flats and Houses (p.13)

1 (a) flat (b) self-contained (c) rent (d) advertisements (e) accommodation agency (f) block (g) fee (h) landlord (i) deposit (j) references **2** (a) terraced (b) cramped (c) spacious (d) estate agent (e) semi-detached (f) surveyor (g) condition (h) removals (i) architect (j) detached (k) builder **3** (a) A landlord owns property and receives rent for it. A tenant pays rent for the use of a room, flat, or other property. (b) A house usually has two or more storeys. A bungalow has only one. (c) The ground floor is at ground level. The first floor is above the ground floor. **4** (a) on (or of) (b) in (c) into (d) with (e) for (f) on (g) in (h) in (i) at … in (j) of

Food and Restaurants (p.14)

1 (a) cookery books (b) dish (c) recipe (d) ingredients (e) snack (f) eat out (g) waiter (h) menu (i) bill (j) tip (k) fast food (l) take-away **2** (a) entertaining (b) cutlery (c) napkin (d) starter (e) main course (f) vegetarian (g) diet (h) side dish (i) dessert (j) washing up (k) sink (l) crockery
3 (a) A buffet: a meal when people help themselves to food laid out on a table, and often eat standing up. A banquet: a grand meal for a lot of people on a special occasion.
(b) Overcooked: cooked too much. Undercooked: not cooked enough. Raw: uncooked:
(c) A chef cooks in a restaurant or hotel. A caterer offers a service providing food and drink for special occasions. (d) A café: a restaurant offering simple meals and snacks. A canteen: a restaurant in a factory, office, school etc. **4** (a) for (b) out (c) down (d) to (e) to (f) to (g) at (h) of (i) out (j) in (k) up

Gambling, Smoking and Drinking (p.15)

1 (a) compulsive gamblers (b) betting (c) games of chance (d) fortune (e) wreck (f) odds (g) bookmakers (h) punters (i) casino (j) broke **2** (a) addiction (b) craving (c) chain-smoke (d) put out (e) antisocial (f) stained (g) ash trays (h) harmful (i) packet (j) fatal **3** (a) soft drinks (b) teetotallers (c) sip (d) sociable (e) spirits (f) tipsy (g) drunk (h) hangover (i) alcoholics (j) sober

Industry and Agriculture (p.16)

1 (a) economy (b) produce (c) products (d) shipyards (e) plants (f) boom (g) slump (h) natural resources (i) import (j) export (k) markets **2** (a) self sufficient (b) farmers (c) dams (d) irrigate (e) fertilizers (f) fertile (g) crops (h) harvest (i) livestock (j) agricultural **3** (a) Oil is extracted from the ground at an oilfield. It is purified and made ready for use at a refinery. (b) Coal or gold etc. are taken from under the ground at a mine. Stone is taken from the surface at a quarry. (c) The producer manufactures goods. The consumer buys them to use. (d) To plough; to break and turn over earth. To sow: to put seeds into ploughed earth. **4** (a) on (b) in (c) of (d) from (e) in (f) to

International Relations (p.17)

1 (a) leader (b) hold (c) summit meeting (d) preliminary (e) agenda (f) item (g) news conference (h) spokesperson (i) breakdown (j) settle **2** (a) split (b) in protest at (c) break off (d) diplomatic relations (e) ambassadors (f) embassies (g) resume (h) links **3** (a) on ... for (b) by (c) at ... in (d) about (e) of (f) in ... at (g) over ... for

Law and Order (p.18)

1 (a) investigate (b) arrest (c) handcuff (d) charge (e) theft (f) fingerprints (g) cell (h) detained (i) court (j) magistrate (k) oath (l) pleaded (m) witnesses (n) evidence (o) found (p) fine (q) sentence **2** (a) solicitor (b) trial ... jury ... verdict (c) warders (d) inquest ... coroner (e) detective ... plain clothes (f) death penalty **3** (a) in (b) to (c) of (d) of (e) with (f) in ... in (g) before (h) of

Music (p.19)

1 (a) concert hall (b) audience (c) musicians (d) instruments (e) conductor (f) bow (g) baton (h) score (i) keys (j) string (k) bows **2** (a) group (b) top ten (c) number one (d) recording studio (e) live (f) concert (g) stage (h) fans (i) vocalist (j) lyrics **3** (a) An orchestra: a large group of musicians, who often play classical music. A band: normally a smaller group, who play popular music. (b) Percussion instruments: played by being hit (drums). Wind instruments: played by being blown (trumpet). (c) A concert: musical performance before an audience. A rehearsal: a practice for a performance. (d) A composer writes music. A musician plays it. **4** (a) at (b) in (c) by (d) on (e) in

Natural Disasters (p.20)

1 (a) drought (b) famine (c) starve (d) starvation (e) flood (f) drown (g) helicopters (h) drop (i) cut off **2** (a) earthquake (b) casualties (c) collapse (d) rescue teams (e) trapped (f) rubble (g) outbreak (h) epidemic (i) medical teams (j) toll **3** (a) on fire (b) fire brigade (c) fire engine (d) fireman (e) overcome (f) under control (g) put out (h) arson **4** (a) of (b) from ... to (c) to ... off (d) for (e) for ... in (f) under (g) by

Public Transport (p.21)

1 (a) cab (b) hail (c) taxi-rank (d) fare (e) meter (f) tip (g) double-decker (h) single-decker (i) crew (j) driver (k) conductor (l) inspector (m) check (n) bus stop (o) destination (p) rush hour (q) tube (r) subway (s) metro (t) platform (u) escalator (v) lift (w) sliding doors (x) coach (y) rack
2 (a) A carriage: separate car or wagon. A compartment: one section of a carriage.
(b) A season ticket enables you to travel as often as you like on a particular route during a given time. A return ticket is only good for one journey each way between two places.
(c) A bus driver drives a bus. A bus conductor collects money for fares. (d) A train driver drives a train. A guard has general responsibility for the safety of the train. **3** (a) in (b) at (c) for (d) for (e) at (f) on (g) at (h) for (i) off … at (j) at (k) from

Romance and Marriage (p.22)

1 (a) romantic (b) attracted (c) keen (d) date (e) go out (f) approve (g) mature (h) drift apart (i) break off (j) relationship **2** (a) propose (b) engaged (c) consent (d) civil (e) wedding (f) bride (g) bridegroom (h) reception (i) toast (j) honeymoon **3** (a) To be fond of someone: to have a warm feeling towards that person. To be in love with someone: have a very deep feeling, often only towards that person. (b) A married couple who are separated live apart. If they are divorced, their marriage is legally at an end. (c) An engaged girl's fiancé is her husband-to-be. An engaged man's fiancée is his wife-to-be. (d) Your mother is the woman who gave birth to you. Your mother-in-law is your husband's or wife's mother. **4** (a) out (b) out with (c) out (d) of (e) to (f) in … with (g) to (h) to (i) of (j) in

Shopping (p.23)

1 flowers; meat; tea, biscuits, butter; writing paper, pens; fruit, vegetables; cigarettes; newspapers, magazines; bread, cakes; dogs, cats; very old furniture **2** (a) off-the-peg (b) label (c) tag (d) fit (e) try on (f) assistant (g) cashier (h) cash desk (i) till (j) receipt (k) exchange (l) refund (m) bargain (n) sales (o) mail order **3** (a) To overcharge: to ask a customer for more than the true price. To undercharge: to ask for less. (b) A shopkeeper owns and runs a shop. A shoplifter steals from shops after entering as a customer. (c) If you go shopping you buy things. If you go window-shopping you just look in the shop-windows. (d) A wholesaler sells goods to retailers. Retailers are shops, which sell to the public. **4** (a) in (b) on (c) at … in (d) by (e) inside (f) back (g) with (h) for

Sport (p.24)

1 (a) pitches (b) courts (c) pools (d) rings (e) rink (f) stadium (g) spectators (h) track events (i) field events (j) athletes (k) officials (l) scoreboard **2** (a) team (b) players (c) amateurs (d) train (e) gymnasium (f) match (g) track suits (h) referee (i) captains (j) toss a coin (k) crowd (l) draw **3** (a) Amateurs are not paid; professionals are paid. (b) A winner wins. A runner-up comes second. (c) You win a game or race. You beat your opponent. (d) A hurdle race has jumps. A relay race has two or more people in the same team, each completing a part of the race. **4** (a) for (b) on (c) on (d) at (e) in (f) of … at (or in) (g) of (h) between (i) in

Television and Newspapers (p.25)

1 (a) mass media (b) switch (c) channels (d) indoctrinate (e) objective (f) subjective (g) commercials (h) soap operas (i) quiz shows (j) viewers **2** (a) advertising (b) circulation (c) entertainment (d) headlines (e) cartoons (f) sensational (g) gossip columns (h) views (i) censorship (j) correspondents (k) news agencies (l) reviews (m) editorials **3** (a) Viewers watch television. Listeners listen to the radio. (b) A mass circulation newspaper sells a large number of copies A small circulation paper sells a small number. (c) An editor runs a newspaper. A reporter writes news stories. A critic reviews new plays, books or films. **4** (a) to (b) for (c) in (d) on

Theatre (p.26)

1 (a) dressing room (b) stage (c) row (d) aisle (e) stalls (f) circle (g) foyer (h) box office (i) backstage (j) box **2** (a) director (b) playwright (c) cast (d) auditions (e) parts (f) audience (g) theatre-goers (h) rehearsals (i) first night (j) applause (k) reviews (l) critics (m) hit (n) run (o) flop (p) performances (q) matinées **3** (a) in (b) to (c) on (d) at (e) in (f) behind (g) during (h) in (i) at … at (j) in

Travel (p.27)

1 (a) leisure (b) travel agents (c) cut-price tickets (d) off the beaten track (e) hitch-hiking (f) youth hostels (g) package holiday (h) resort (i) peak (j) off-peak **2** (a) travel (b) journey (c) tour (d) cruise (e) voyage (f) trip (g) flight (h) journey (i) tour (j) trip **3** (a) A bed and breakfast place is a cheap, simple hotel where the overnight charge includes breakfast. (b) People are seasick in ships, airsick when flying and carsick in cars if the movement upsets their stomach. (c) A tour operator organises holidays. A travel agent sells them to the public. (d) At sea: on a ship far from land. At the seaside: by the sea, often at a holiday coastal resort. **4** (a) by (b) in (c) on (d) in (e) at

War (p.28)

1 (a) clashes (b) forces (c) aggression (d) mobilise (e) hostile acts (f) retaliate (g) deteriorate (h) ultimatum (i) declare war (j) outbreak **2** (a) civilian (b) targets (c) neutral (d) intermediary (e) get involved (f) intervene (g) ceasefire (h) peace-keeping force (i) peace treaty (j) withdraw **3** (a) An army advances when it goes forward against the enemy and retreats when it goes back under enemy pressure. (b) War: usually between two or more countries. Civil war: between two sides in the same country. (c) Conventional war: fought with troops and 'ordinary' weapons (guns, ships, planes). Nuclear war: fought with nuclear weapons. (d) An ally: a group or country which fights on your side. An enemy: the side opposing you. **4** (a) on (b) in ... for (c) in (d) out (e) as ... in (f) out (g) between

Welfare State (p.29)

1 (a) welfare state (b) elderly (c) pension (d) retire (e) low incomes (f) subsidised (g) medical treatment (h) benefits (i) schooling (j) physically disabled (k) mentally handicapped (l) out of work (m) eligible (n) social services (o) social workers **2** (a) Advice: a noun. Advise: a verb. (b) Blind: unable to see. Deaf: partially or totally unable to hear. (c) Free: without charge. Subsidised: (rent, meals, food) of lower price than is normal because the government or company pays a part. (d) A hearing aid helps the deaf to hear. Braille helps the blind to read. (e) Haves: people who have money, jobs, homes. Have-nots: people who lack these. **3** (a) with (b) out of (c) in ... for (d) at (or in) (e) at ... of (f) for

Work (p.30)

1 (a) applicants (b) vacancy (c) fill in (d) application forms (e) apply (f) short-list (g) interview (h) qualifications (i) experience (j) references **2** (a) salary (b) increments (c) pension (d) retire (e) commission (f) perks (g) prospects (h) promotion (i) commute (j) ambitious **3** (a) in (b) at (c) to ... for ... as (d) for (e) in (f) in (g) in (h) at (i) of (j) of (k) to

Mini topics

Argument (p.31)

(a) resentment (b) friction (c) jealous (d) row (e) disagreement (f) troublemaker (g) aggressive (h) nag

Sadness (p.31)

(a) tears (b) sob (c) heartbroken (d) loss (e) comfort (f) grief (g) sleepless (h) recover (i) withdrawn (j) miss

Nervousness (p.31)

(a) nerves (b) tremble (c) sweat (d) blush (e) embarrassment (f) shy (g) tongue-tied (h) stammer (i) faint (j) tranquillizer

Success (p.32)

(a) ambitious (b) ladder (c) power (d) achieve (e) achievement (f) confidence (g) exploit (h) ruthless (i) determined (j) ability

Fame (p.32)

(a) celebrity (b) entourage (c) autographs (d) fans (e) interviews (f) in the public eye (g) privacy (h) bodyguards (i) pressures (j) break-up

Pride (p.32)

(a) snob (b) proud (c) contemptuous (d) boast (e) vain (f) conceited (g) thick-skinned (h) pride

Birth (p.33)

(a) expecting (b) pregnant (c) born (d) maternity ward (e) midwife (f) deliver (g) parents (h) call (i) prams (j) cots (k) crawl

Childhood and Adolescence (p.33)

(a) adults (b) adult (c) daydreams (d) idolise (e) hobbies (f) teens (g) development (h) introverts (i) extroverts (j) relationships

Death (p.33)

(a) hearse (b) funeral (c) priest (d) dead (e) mourners (f) cemetery (g) crematorium (h) will (i) leave (j) widow (k) inherits

Advertising (p.34)

(a) classified advertisements (b) posters (c) hoardings (d) advertising agencies (e) publicise (f) eye-catching (g) commercials (h) persuade

Art (p.34)

(a) creative (b) sculptor (c) sculpture (d) painter (e) amateur (f) professional (g) dealers (h) works (i) galleries (j) reproductions

Photograph (p.34)

(a) camera (b) snaps (c) prints (d) album (e) slides (f) projector (g) develop (h) enlargements

Military Service (p.34)

(a) compulsory (b) forces (c) volunteers (d) army (e) navy (f) air force (g) promotion (h) officer

Police (p.35)

(a) join (b) police force (c) policeman (d) rank (e) uniform (f) walkie-talkie (g) detective (h) plain clothes

Security Work (p.35)

(a) security firm (b) armoured vehicles (c) bullet-proof (d) guards (e) tap (f) bug (g) private detectives (h) couriers (i) kidnappers

The Countryside (p.35)

(a) rural (b) unpolluted (c) pace (d) villages (e) relaxed (f) cultivated (g) farms (h) national parks (i) wildlife (j) remote

Street English (p.35)

I don't know. Thats OK. What are you doing? Here he is. Who's that?

The Seaside (p.36)

(a) beach (b) horizon (c) waves (d) drown (e) currents (f) depth (g) lifeguards (h) dive (i) shallow (j) cliffs

Mountains (p.36)

(a) range (b) height (c) ascent (d) mountaineers (e) climb (f) peak (g) oxygen (h) equipment (i) ropes (j) descent

Electrical Appliances (p.36)

(a) lead (b) plug (c) socket (d) switch (e) adjust (f) knob (g) controls (h) unplug (i) electrician (j) dealer

The Telephone (p.37)

(a) operator (b) look up (c) directory (d) receiver (e) dial (f) engaged (g) get through (h) line

Computers (p.37)

(a) calculator (b) computers (c) hardware (d) software (e) screen (f) keyboard (g) printer (h) word processor

Factory Work (p.37)

(a) manual (b) white collar (c) apprentice (d) factory (e) foreman (f) canteen (g) tea break (h) labour relations (i) management (j) shop floor

Office Work (p.38)

(a) correspondence (b) file (c) filing cabinets (d) callers (e) dictate (f) shorthand (g) typewriter (h) stationery

A Strike (p.38)

(a) go on strike (b) dispute (c) dismiss (d) shop steward (e) deadlock (f) unemployment (g) on the dole (h) picket line (i) redundant

Related Word Groups

Sounds (p.39)

1 (a) squeal (b) crash (c) roar (d) rustle (e) splash (f) bang (g) creak (h) whistle (i) clatter (j) rumble **2** (a) hum (b) pips (c) pop (d) crack (e) peal (f) squeak (g) tick (h) jingle

Animal Sounds (p.40)

(a) chatter (b) roar (c) bark, growl (d) miaow, purr (e) neigh (f) cluck (g) crow (h) buzz (i) moo (j) bleat (k) trumpet (l) grunt, squeal (m) bray (n) croak (o) hiss (p) quack (q) howl (r) squeak

Human Sounds (p.40)

(a) stammer (b) sniff (c) puff ... pant (d) snore (e) hiccup (f) sneeze (g) whisper (h) yawn (i) sigh (j) cough (k) groan

Ways of Looking (p.41)

(a) stare (b) peep (c) blink (d) gaze (e) frown (f) glimpse (g) wink (h) peer (i) glare (j) glance

Walking (p.41)

(a) stagger (b) wander (c) stroll (d) limp (e) slip (f) creep (g)march (h) stray (i) crawl (j) trip (k) dash (l) trudge

Body Movements (p.42)

1 (a) his muscles ... (b) his head in disagreement ... (c) his fists (d) his neck ... (e) his fingers ... (f) his shoulders ... (g) his forehead ... (h) his arms ... (i) his head thoughtfully ... (j) his breath ... (k) his foot ... (l) his knee ... **2** (a) with fear (b) with cold (c) in the hot sun (d) with embarrassment (e) when he heard the sad news (f) in surprise at the sudden noise (g) in his armchair after a hard day's work (h) after going without food for three days **3** (a) in agreement (b) when he was introduced to the Queen (c) when she was introduced to the Queen (d) when she saw her friend getting off the bus (e) because he was happy (f) when his commanding officer entered the room (g) after sitting in the same position for so long (h) to show the shop assistant what he wanted **4** (a) stretch (b) slap (c) punch (d) pat (e) stroke (f) grab (g) squeeze (h) grope (i) nudge (j) beckon

Containers (p.43)

(a) shopping (b) clothes and personal things for a long stay (c) petrol, water (d) cash, secret documents, jewellery (e) flowers (f) coins (g) bank notes, tickets (h) boiling water (i) suits, jackets, dresses (j) business papers (k) letter (l) water, milk (m) clothes and belongings for, say, a week's holiday (n) beer (o) school books (p) waste paper (q) chocolates, matches (r) hot tea, cold drinks

Furniture and Fittings (p.44)

(a) curtains (b) cupboard (c) bookcase (d) shelf (e) cushion (f) sofa (g) desk (h) chair (i) carpet (j) armchair (k) table (l) lampshade (m) lamp (n) drawer (o) pillow (p) sheet (q) wardrobe (r) blanket (s) mattress (t) rug (u) stool (v) washbasin (w) bed (x) chest of drawers

Connectors (p.45)

1 (a) nut (b) screw (c) needle (d) nail (e) pin (f) bolt (g) safety pin (h) drawing pin (i) chain (j) rope (k) paper clip (l) string (m) thread (n) rubber band **2** (a) needle … thread (b) string (c) rope (d) safety pins (e) nail (f) drawing spin (g) pins (h) paper clip (i) nuts … bolts (j) screws (k) chains (l) rubber band

Tools (p.46)

1 (a) hammer (b) spanner (c) screwdriver (d) axe (e) penknife (f) chisel (g) scissors (h) mallet (i) jack (j) rake (k) drill (l) saw (m) spade (n) fork **2** (a) scissors (b) screwdriver (c) spade (d) drill (e) jack (f) hammer (g) axe (h) chisel (i) mallet (j) rake (k) penknife (l) fork (m) saw (n) spanner

Vehicles (p.47)

(a) motorbike (b) van (c) bulldozer (d) scooter (e) lorry (f) caravan (g) tanker (h) trailer (i) car (j) ambulance (k) bus (l) coach

Bicycle (p.47)

(a) saddle (b) frame (c) back light (d) mudguard (e) gears (f) chain (g) pedal (h) pump (i) spokes (j) tyre (k) front light (l) handlebars (m) brakes (n) bell

Collective Nouns (p.48)

(a) fleet (b) herd (c) swarm (d) mob (e) suite (f) crowd (g) bunch (h) congregation (i) shoals (j) flight (k) gang (l) clump (m) flocks (n) swarm (o) bunch (p) fleet (q) bundle (r) audience (s) bunch (t) set (u) stack (v) suite (w) pack (x) crew (y) flock (z) set

Misprints (p.48)

aunt (ant), card (car), car (cat), windows (widows), sunny (funny)

Young Animals (p.49)

(a) cub (b) foal (c) piglet (d) cub (e) puppy (f) calf (g) kitten (h) cub (i) duckling (j) lamb (k) kid (l) chick

Law Breakers (p.49)

1 (a) sets fire to property … (b) steals from shops … (c) attacks and robs people … (d) is anyone who breaks the law (e) deliberately causes damage to property (f) breaks into houses … (g) kills someone (h) takes away people by force … (i) steals things from people's pockets … (j) helps a criminal … (k) buys and sells drugs … (l) gets secret information from another country (m) uses violence for political reasons **2** (a) murders … (b) causes damage or disturbance … (c) hides on a ship … (d) is someone who steals (e) takes control of a plane … (f) makes counterfeit money … (g) steals money etc. by force … (h) brings goods into a country illegally … (i) betrays his or her country … (j) is a member of a criminal group (k) is a soldier who runs away from the army (l) marries illegally …

Occupations (p.50)

1 (a) controls parking … (b) collects rubbish … (c) arranges shop-window displays (d) helps people buy and sell houses (e) deals with office correspondence … (f) makes arrangements for funerals (g) makes brick buildings and walls (h) works in a government ministry (i) treats sick animals (j) sells newspapers … (k) delivers babies **2** (a) cooks in a restaurant … (b) designs buildings (c) works in a library (d) sells fish … (e) gets coal … (f) runs a museum (g) designs the insides of houses … (h) types letters … (i) drives someone's car … (j) operates on sick people **3** (a) tests people's eyes … (b) make people laugh at a circus (c) rides racehorses (d) sells valuable objects at an auction (e) prepares books … for publication (f) loads and unloads ships … (g) treats people's feet (h) sells meat (i) writes for a newspaper (j) represents country … (k) sells flowers …

Male and Female (p.51)

(a) queen (b) wife (c) bride (d) hero (e) girl guide (f) barman (g) policeman (h) air stewardess (or hostess) (i) headmaster (j) monk (k) waitress (l) prince (m) niece (n) actor (o) hostess (p) landlady (q) widower (r) uncle

People (p.51)

(a) can't stop talking (b) is intellectual … (c) is inquisitive … (d) loves reading books (e) is very keen on the cinema (f) is slow (g) is not very active or energetic (h) is confused and forgetful (i) loves to work (j) likes to open the windows … (k) is clever and ambitious … (l) causes difficulties between people (m) seems to enjoy preventing others from enjoying themselves

Clothes (p.52)

1 (a) shirt (b) tie (c) jacket (d) waistcoat (e) overcoat (f) trousers (g) shoes (h) boots (i) suits (j) pullover (k) blouse (l) scarf (m) hat (n) cap (o) tee-shirt (p) shorts (q) sandals (r) socks (s) pyjamas (t) dress (u) slippers (v) apron (w) skirt **2** (a) lining (b) lapel (c) sleeve (d) pocket (e) toe (f) laces (g) heel (h) sole (i) collar (j) label (k) seam (l) cuff (m) button (n) belt (o) crease (p) zip (q) buckle **3** (a) dress (b) dresses (c) wear (d) dressed (e) wearing (f) dressed (g) dress (h) wearing … dress (i) dress (j) dress **4** (a) up (b) off (c) on (d) in (e) up (f) on (g) off … on (h) in (i) up (j) up

Parts of the Body (p.54)

1 (a) forehead (b) hair (c) eye (d) ear (e) cheek (f) nostril (g) mouth (h) throat (i) chin (j) neck (k) jaw (l) lips (m) nose (n) eyelashes (o) eyelid (p) eyebrow **2** (a) shoulder (b) arm (c) hand (d) leg (e) foot (f) sole (g) toe (h) heel (i) ankle (j) shin (k) calf (l) knee (m) thigh (n) nail (o) finger (p) palm (q) thumb (r) hip (s) wrist (t) waist (u) forearm (v) elbow (w) stomach (x) chest

Punctuation Marks and Printing (p.55)

(a) capital letter (b) small letter (c) stroke (d) dash (e) heading (f) hyphen (g) semicolon (h) paragraph (i) full stop (j) italics (k) bracket (l) apostrophe (m) question mark (n) inverted commas (o) abbreviation (p) footnote (q) asterisk (r) exclamation mark (s) subheading (t) comma (u) colon (v) underlining

British Measurements (p.56)

(a) inch (b) foot (c) yard (d) mile (e) acre (f) ounce (g) pound (h) stone (i) pint (j) gallon

Quantities (p.56)

(a) of soap (b) of shoes (c) of matches (d) of potatoes (e) of film (f) of tobacco (g) of cloth (h) of milk (i) of land (j) of wine (k) of petrol (l) of flowers (m) of sardines (n) of toothpaste (o) of cigarettes (p) of jam

Shapes (p.57)

(a) shape (b) size (c) rectangle (d) horizontal (e) vertical (f) square (g) diagonal (h) centre (i) corner (j) triangle (k) angle (l) right angle (m) parallel (n) upper (o) lower (p) circle

Britain and the British Isles (pp.58-59)

1 England	**2** Scotland	**3** Wales	**4** N. Ireland	**5** Rep. of Ireland
6 Cornwall	**7** W. Country	**8** Home Counties	**9** E. Anglia	**10** Midlands
11 Irish Sea	**12** Channel	**13** North Sea	**14** Bristol Channel	**15** John O'Groats
16 Edinburgh	**17** Glasgow	**18** Newcastle	**19** Blackpool	**20** Manchester

21 Liverpool	22 Birmingham	23 Cambridge	24 Stratford-on-Avon	25 Cardiff
26 Bristol	27 Bath	28 Oxford	29 Windsor	30 London
31 Canterbury	32 Dover	33 Brighton	34 Belfast	35 Dublin
36 Loch Ness	37 Loch Lomond	38 R. Clyde	39 Isle of Man	40 R. Severn
41 R. Avon	42 R. Thames	43 Isle of Wight	44 Shetlands	45 Orkneys
46 Hebrides	47 Scilly Isles	48 Channel Isles	49 Snowdonia	50 Ben Nevis
51 Highlands	52 Lake District	53 Pennines	54 Yorkshire Moors	55 Peak District
56 Cotswolds	57 Dartmoor	58 Land's End	59 Salisbury Plain	60 Fens
61 The Wash				

Word Building

Prefixes (pp. 60–62)

1 (a) co (b) inter (c) co (d) ex (e) inter (f) re (g) inter (h) re (i) ex (j) co **2** (a) counter (b) bi (c) pre (d) semi (e) bi (f) bi (g) pre (h) counter (i) semi (j) semi **3** (a) post (b) non (c) mono (d) non (e) post (f) mono (g) anti (h) anti (i) non **4** (a) de (b) trans (c) de (d) super (e) trans (f) multi (g) de (h) super (i) super (j) multi **5** (a) sub (b) pro (c) sub (d) sub (e) uni (f) tri (g) pro (h) tri (i) pro (j) uni **6** (a) over (b) over (c) under (d) over (e) under (f) under (g) over (h) under (i) over (j) under **7** (a) un (b) un (c) un (d) dis (e) un (f) dis (g) un (h) un (i) dis (j) un (k) dis (l) un (m) dis (n) dis (o) dis (p) un (q) dis (r) dis (s) dis (t) un (u) dis (v) dis **8** (a) ir (b) im (c) il (d) in (e) im (f) im (g) in (h) il (i) ir (j) im (k) in (l) ir (m) im (n) il (o) in (p) il (q) in (r) ir (s) in (t) in (u) ir (v) in

Suffixes (pp.63–65)

1 (i) (a) monkish (b) amateurish (c) childish (d) piggish (e) girlish (ii) (a) sevenish (b) darkish (c) fairish (d) twentyish (e) tallish (f) smallish (g) greenish **2** (a) waterless (b) harmful (c) thoughtful (d) successful (e) harmless (f) thoughtless (g) beautiful (h) friendless **3** (a) employer (b) trainer (c) interviewer … interviewee (d) employee (e) trainee **4** (a) bulletproof (b) waterproof (c) shockproof (d) heatproof (e) foolproof (f) childproof (g) soundproof **5** (a) cupful … teaspoonful (b) houseful (c) handful (d) mouthful (e) tankful **6** (a) teacher (b) director (c) beggar (d) interpreter (e) translator (f) collector (g) sailor (h) murderer (i) operator (j) demonstrator (k) inspector (l) actor (m) buyer (n) editor (o) worker (p) donor (q) visitor (r) producer (s) traveller (t) competitor **7** (a) singer (b) governor (c) announcer (d) admirer (e) decorator (f) robber (g) survivor (h) supplier (i) controller (j) investigator (k) skier (l) instructor (m) elector (n) writer (o) photographer (p) swimmer (q) contributor (r) creator (s) manager (t) liar **8** (a) motorist (b) electrician (c) Parisian (d) Christian (e) pianist (f) historian (g) Buddhist (h) economist (i) artist (j) cyclist (k) guitarist (l) politician (m) scientist (n) musician (o) psychiatrist (p) terrorist (q) magician (r) florist (s) comedian (t) beautician (u) journalist (v) parachutist (w) linguist (x) archaeologist

Nouns made from Verbs (pp.66–73)

1 (a) diagnosis (b) enclosure (c) analysis (d) hypnosis (e) failure (f) signature (g) emphasis (h) seizure (i) paralysis (j) closure **2** (a) delivery (b) injury (c) forgery (d) recovery (e) discovery (f) prosperity (g) Assembly (h) apology (i) conspiracy (j) expiry (k) enquiry **3** (a) correspondence (b) defence (c) obedience (d) preference (e) pretence (f) reference (g) dependence (h) existence (i) insistence (j) difference (k) offence (l) coincidence (m) interference (n) residence **4** (a) performance (b) attendance (c) resemblance (d) acceptance (e) disturbance (f) insurance (g) assistance (h) annoyance (i) entrance (j) resistance (k) endurance (l) avoidance **5** (a) dismissal (b) burial (c) arrival (d) renewal (e) approval (f) rehearsal (g) trial (h) proposal (i) survival (j) denial (k) refusal (l) removal **6** (a) storage (b) passage (c) marriage (d) stoppage (e) postage (f) wreckage (g) leakage (h) usage (i) breakage (j) shrinkage **7** (a) advice (b) practice (c) licence (d) prophecy (e) choice (f) behaviour (g) complaint (h) error (i) loss (j) mixture (k) growth **8** (a) censorship (b) death (c) conquest (d) belief (e) proof (f) relief (g) remainder (h) remains (i) reminder (j) prayer (k) comparison **9** (a) pursuit (b) hatred (c) ascent … descent (d) ruins (e) contents (f) knowledge (g) decision (h) tendency (i) suspicion (j) applause (k) service (l) weight (m) threat (n) shot (o) robbery (p) response **10** (a) persuasion (b) division (c) expansion (d) admission (e) explosion (f) revision (g) inclusion (h) exclusion

(i) conclusion **11** (a) invasion (b) collision (c) permission (d) impression (e) possession (f) confession (g) confusion (h) discussion (i) extension **12** (a) arrangement (b) enlargement (c) entertainment (d) postponement (e) improvement (f) encouragement (g) advertisement **13** (a) government (b) punishment (c) management … agreement (d) employment (e) treatment (f) disappointment (g) imprisonment (h) announcement (i) development **14** (a) competition (b) pronunciation (c) qualification (d) production (e) solution (f) introduction (g) acquisition (h) revolution (i) repetition (j) reduction **15** (a) destruction (b) opposition (c) publication (d) reception (e) deception (f) abolition (g) explanation (h) detention (i) satisfaction (j) description **16** (a) interruption (b) prediction … election (c) reaction (d) Prevention (e) invention (f) addiction (g) Protection (h) suggestion (i) selection **17** (a) investigation (b) exaggeration (c) operation (d) imitation (e) pronunciation (f) resignation (g) foundation (h) communication (i) imagination (j) accusation (k) cancellation (l) admiration (m) abbreviation (n) preparation (o) demonstration (p) education (q) emigration (r) immigration **18** (a) donation (b) hesitation (c) acceleration (d) reservation (e) sensation (f) combination (g) interrogation (h) invitation (i) deterioration (j) examination (k) alteration (l) information (m) relaxation (n) restoration (o) temptation (p) continuation (q) exploration (r) translation (s) interpretation (t) punctuation

Euphemisms (p.76)

died, lying, is unwell, go to the toilet, drank too much

Nouns made from Adjectives (pp.74–77)

1 (a) wealth (b) Poverty (c) truth (d) thirst (e) hunger (f) ease (g) youth (h) gratitude (i) likelihood (j) health (k) guilt (l) freedom **2** (a) death (b) cowardice (c) heroism (d) wisdom (e) anger (f) fame (g) splendour (h) boredom (i) horror (j) heat (k) pride (l) strength **3** (a) luck (b) warmth (c) terror (d) length (e) width (f) height (g) depth **4** (a) violence (b) silence (c) confidence (d) elegance (e) innocence (f) importance (g) intelligence (h) arrogance (i) independence (j) reluctance (k) patience (l) convenience (m) absence (n) presence **5** (a) accuracy (b) vacancy (c) urgency (d) obstinacy (e) fluency (f) efficiency (g) frequency (h) privacy **6** (a) baldness (b) foolishness (c) punctuality (d) equality (e) deafness (f) popularity (g) quietness (h) similarity **7** (a) seriousness (b) Christianity (c) neatness (d) superiority (e) neutrality (f) bluntness (g) illness (h) formality (i) weakness (j) fondness (k) reality (l) stupidity **8** (a) clarity (b) necessity (c) brevity (d) curiosity (e) anxiety (f) generosity (g) simplicity (h) vanity (i) variety (j) gaiety **9** (a) courtesy (b) Cruelty (c) beauty (d) jealousy … envy (e) safety (f) tragedy (g) difficulty (h) royalty (i) fury (j) hypocrisy (k) certainty (l) loyalty **10** (a) loneliness (b) ugliness (c) happiness (d) laziness (e) holiness (f) naughtiness (g) tidiness (h) loveliness **11** (a) tension (b) perfection (c) contentment (d) caution (e) excitement (f) attraction

Adjectives made from Nouns (pp.78–79)

1 (a) scholarly (b) rainy (c) grassy (d) friendly (e) salty (f) ghostly (g) yearly (h) weekly **2** (a) poisonous (b) religious (c) adventurous (d) nervous (e) mountainous (f) humorous (g) miraculous (h) dangerous (i) glorious (j) ambitious (k) courageous (l) disastrous (m) famous (n) industrious (o) infectious (p) mysterious (q) victorious (r) suspicious **3** (a) alcoholic (b) artistic (c) climatic (d) democratic (e) energetic (f) photographic (g) scientific (h) sympathetic (i) poetic (j) dramatic **4** (a) grammatical (b) alphabetical (c) musical (d) practical (e) theatrical (f) political (g) psychological (h) medical (i) critical (j) clerical **5** (a) fashionable (b) triumphant (c) affectionate (d) circular (e) literary (f) suburban (g) triangular (h) troublesome (i) comfortable (j) profitable (k) muscular (l) valuable (m) skilful (or skilled) (n) socialist (o) successful (p) trustworthy (or trusted) (q) peaceful (r) memorable (s) knowledgeable (t) distant

Adjectives made from Verbs (p.80)

1 (a) advisable (b) changeable (c) regrettable (d) suitable (e) dependable (f) breakable (g) readable (h) adjustable (i) enjoyable (j) acceptable (k) agreeable (l) curable **2** (a) appreciative (b) productive (c) deceptive (d) destructive (e) informative (f) creative (g) attractive (h) talkative (i) protective (j) decisive **3** (a) dead (b) boring (c) economical (d) quarrelsome (e) introductory (f) entertaining (g) observant (h) obedient (i) residential (j) slippery (k) educational (l) spoilt (m) sticky (n) explanatory

Verbs made from Nouns (p.81)

(a) encourage (b) extend (c) frighten (d) relieve (e) bleed (f) prove (g) endanger (h) identify (i) strengthen (j) liberate (k) breathe (l) halve (m) lengthen

Verbs made from Adjectives (p.81)

(a) brighten (b) lessen (c) ripen (d) sweeten (e) worsen (f) widen (g) loosen (h) lighten (i) deafen (j) flatten (k) darken (l) deepen (m) sharpen (n) broaden (o) quieten (p) straighten (q) tighten (r) weaken

Specialised Vocabulary

Formal Words (pp.82–83)

1 (a) produce (b) stating (c) attend (d) obligatory (e) facilitate (f) seek (g) enquire (h) admitted (i) leave **2** (a) held (b) in possession of (c) prior (d) additional (e) terminating (f) in excess of (g) desire (h) retain (i) notify (j) locations (k) provide (l) further **3** (a) in duration (b) commences (c) departs (d) prior to (e) commencement (f) ensure (g) funds (h) undertake (i) assist (j) requested (k) appropriate (l) attire **4** (a) enquire (b) facilitate (c) prior (d) prior (e) assist (f) in excess of (g) additional (h) notify (i) commencement (j) funds (k) retain (l) provide (m) hold (n) terminate (o) attend (p) admitted (q) state (r) desire (s) leave (t) produce (u) ensure (v) requested

Slang and Colloquial Words (p.84)

1 (a) cigarettes (b) pounds … alcohol (c) made (d) without money (e) friend … prison (f) discarded (g) television … nuisance (h) policeman **2** (a) dismiss (b) very good (c) upper class (d) child … bicycle (e) short sleep (f) joking (g) toilet (h) without money (i) drunk (j) newspaper (k) possessions

Idioms from Sports and Games (p.86)

neck and neck: absolutely level, hot favourite: most popular to win, odds: chances of winning, low blow: unfair move, down and out: poor, homeless and destitute, opening rounds: first in a series, to weather the storm: to overcome a crisis, plain sailing: easy, uncomplicated, stalemate: position in which neither party in a dispute can take steps against each other, checkmate: a move which puts an end to a rival's plans, pawn: person of minor importance who is manipulated by stronger forces, put all your cards on the table: to make one's intentions clear, poker-face: a face that shows no expression, last lap: last part of a course of action, bull's-eye: target, set your sights on: to aim for, kick-off: the start

American Words (p.87)

1 (a) playing truant … fail (b) tap … flat … caretaker (c) rise … holidays (d) postman … trousers (e) railway timetable (f) ordinary uniformed policeman … saloon car … pavement (g) chemist … nappies (h) bill (i) post **2** (a) queue … cinema (b) garden … autumn (c) specialise … maths (mathematics) … university … secondary school (d) petrol … petrol station … windscreen (e) shops … underground (f) lift … ground floor (g) sweets … jam (h) note (i) rubbish

Newspaper Headlines (p.88)

1 (a) close down … (b) attempt (c) explosion (d) fire (e) conflict … (f) reduce … (g) exciting or dramatic event (h) diplomat (i) affect badly (j) vote … (k) investigate … (l) leave … (m) question … (n) mystery (o) look for … (p) reduce drastically (q) angry argument (r) total number of dead (s) marry (t) attract … **2** (a) The army has closed down three bases and dismissed 2,000 men to save money. (b) An attempt to reach the North Pole has failed. (c) Eight people have been killed in an explosion at a hotel. (d) Some animals have died in a fire at a zoo. (e) The United States and Russia are in disagreement about arms reductions. (f) Three people have been saved in a dramatic fire at a block of flats. (g) A diplomat has been accused of spying. (h) Tourists have been badly affected by a pilots' strike. (i) The Prime

Minister has announced that there will be elections in March. (j) The police are investigating the mystery of a missing woman. (k) A leading scientist has left the United Kingdom to move to the United States. (l) Three people have been questioned (by the police) about the kidnapping of a boy. (m) A film star wants a divorce. (n) Air fares have been drastically reduced to attract more holidaymakers to fly. (o) There has been an argument at the United Nations about an accusation that certain people are spies. (p) The total number of people who died in the earthquake is now 27. (q) An actor is going to marry for the fifth time.

Abbreviations (pp.89–90)

1 (a) BBC (b) NSPCC (c) RSPCA (d) AA (e) C of E (f) MI5 (g) BR (h) OHMS (i) BA (j) M4 (k) ITV (l) lb ... oz (m) ft ... ins (n) Esq ... c/o ... Rd **2** (a) UN (b) EU (c) OPEC (d) CIA (e) NATO (f) FBI (g) US (h) UK **3** (a) PTO (b) v (c) Bros ... St (d) BC (e) °F ... °C (f) AD (g) RSVP (h) PS (i) No (j) CD (k) PIN

Classified Advertisements (pp.91–92)

1 (a) bed-sit (b) own ckng facilities (c) to let (d) c.h. (e) fully-furn (f) b/w.c. (g) inc. g/elec (h) labour-saving (i) self-contained (j) handy tube (k) lounge (l) suit **2** (a) m/f 17+ (b) ann. bonus (c) pens scheme (d) commission (e) c.v. (f) ann. increments (g) ann., p.a. (h) references (i) shopping discount (j) fringe benefits (k) negotiable (l) good prospects (m) + **3** (a) fly-drive (b) self-catering (c) cmpng (d) B&B (e) half-board (f) full-board (g) SAE (h) all-inclusive (i) overland (j) off-peak **4** (a) sec hnd (b) upholstery (c) Gent's (d) accessories (e) weekdays (f) low mileage (g) good m.p.g. (h) ex-demonstration (i) free estimate (j) refs. available (k) o.n.o. (l) fully gurntd (m) shop-soiled (n) byr to collect

Shortened Words (p.93)

1 photo, mac, motor-bike, gym, paper, hippo, phone, plane, car, taxi, bike, kilo, pop, pub, zoo, exam, vet, fax **2** advertisement, limousine, nightgown, demonstration, laboratory, doctor, microphone, spectacles, comfortable, liberation, champion, professional

Problem Pairs (pp.94–98)

Pairs of Words Often Confused

1 (a) lose (b) loose (c) lose (d) loose **2** (a) their (b) their (c) there (d) there **3** (a) advise (b) advice (c) advice (d) advise **4** (a) whether (b) weather (c) weather (d) whether **5** (a) beside (b) beside (c) besides (d) besides **6** (a) stationary (b) stationery (c) stationary (d) stationery **7** (a) agree (b) accept (c) agree (d) accept **8** (a) understanding (b) comprehensive (c) comprehensive (d) understanding **9** (a) sensible (b) sensitive (c) sensible (d) sensitive ... sensitive **10** (a) now (b) now (c) actually (d) actually **11** (a) control (b) check (c) control (d) check **12** (a) teacher (b) teacher (c) professor (d) Professor **13** (a) effect (b) affect (c) affect (d) effect **14** (a) passed (b) passed (c) past (d) past **15** (a) economical (b) economic (c) economic (d) economical **16** (a) principles (b) principle (c) principal (d) principal **17** (a) grateful (b) thankful (c) thankful (d) grateful **18** (a) lend (b) borrow (c) borrow (d) lend **19** (a) quiet (b) quite (c) quiet (d) quite **20** (a) Canal (b) canals (c) Channel (d) channel **21** (a) valueless (b) priceless (c) priceless (d) valueless **22** (a) invaluable (b) invaluable (c) worthless (d) worthless **23** (a) continually (b) continuously (c) continuously (d) continually **24** (a) hard (b) hard (c) hardly (d) hardly **25** (a) avoid (b) prevent (c) prevent (d) avoid **26** (a) raised (b) rise (c) rose (d) raised (e) rise (f) raised (g) raised (h) risen (i) rises (j) raised **27** (a) stole (b) robbed (c) robbed (d) stolen (e) stolen (f) rob (g) stole (h) robbed (i) stole **28** (a) lies (b) laid (c) Lay (d) lay (e) lain (f) lay (g) lie (h) laid (i) lying (j) lay (k) laid (l) lay ... lie **29** (a) remember (b) remind (c) remember (d) remember (e) reminded (f) remind (g) remember (h) remind (i) remember (j) reminds

One Word or Two? (p.99)

(a) may be (b) Maybe (c) alright (d) all right (e) altogether (f) all together (g) some times (h) Sometimes (i) already (j) all ready (k) Everyone (l) every one (m) anyone (n) any one (o) no body (p) Nobody (q) everyday (r) every day

Word Games (p.104)

2 Many answers are possible: are-era, dam-mad, saw-was, ten-net, won-now, laid-dial, liar-rail, pets-step, wolf-flow, stink-knits, reward-drawer, desserts-stressed etc. **3** Other answers possible: certain, soldier, slower, bones, leaves, often, holding **5** Occupations: carpenter, policeman, actor, doctor, lawyer, teacher, footballer, politician. Countries: Argentina, Indonesia, Belgium, Bolivia, Algeria, England, New Zealand, South Africa. Clothing: underwear, overcoat, sweater, blouse, raincoat, trousers, pullover, jacket **7** missed, bare, brake, site, sighs, aisle, week, pane, sea, sore, flour, prince **8** (a) egg-cup, backbone, lighthouse, pocket money, river-bank, doormat, tin opener (b) teaspoon, fire-engine, paper-clip, sports-car, toothpaste, hour hand, sea-bed **9** Other answers possible: beer, slow, bright, care, stick, she, black, hear, east, scare, send, where, smile, shot, swear, plane, chat, neat **10** Grandma always had a bad back. I think I'll hit him if he's silly again. They think it's better to take a train. She says she saw someone steal some scissors. Only one or two boys know who wrote the note. The three very well-dressed women went there every Wednesday. **11** (a) earth (b) right (c) firm (d) part (e) anxious (f) kind (g) fly (h) back (i) admit (j) funny (k) engaged (l) try (m) dear (n) sole (o) safe (p) curious (q) leave (r) fair (s) sign (t) cross